Education Write Now, Volume II

In this innovative series *Education Write Now*, ten of education's most inspiring thought-leaders meet for a three-day retreat to think and write collaboratively, and then bring you the top takeaways you need right now to improve your school or classroom.

This second volume, edited by Jeff Zoul and Sanée Bell, focuses on relationships—the heart of everything we do in education. Building strong relationships and a positive school culture takes intentional, consistent effort, and the authors provide strategies and examples to help you along the way.

Throughout the book, you'll find insights and inspiration on these topics:

- Connecting the dots among students and staff (Jeffrey Zoul)
- Strengthening relationships in the learner-centered class (Randy Ziegenfuss)
- Building a culture of equity and access (Rosa Isiah)
- Cultivating student strengths and interests (Elisabeth Bostwick)
- Bridging the gap between schools and families (Laura Gilchrist)
- Deepening connections through productive conflict (Sanée Bell)
- Finding relationships beyond the four walls (Onica Mayers)
- Connecting through the power of generosity (Winston Sakurai)
- Bringing passion into the schoolhouse (Sean Gaillard)
- Tapping into dreams for a world-class culture (Danny Bauer)

The royalties generated from this book will support the Will to Live Foundation, a nonprofit foundation working to prevent teen suicide.

Jeffrey Zoul (@jeff_zoul) is a lifelong teacher, learner, and leader. During Jeff's distinguished career in education he has served in a variety of roles, most recently as Assistant Superintendent for Teaching and Learning with Deerfield Public Schools District 109 in Illinois. Jeff also served as a teacher and coach in Georgia before moving into school administration. He has authored many books, including *What Connected Educators Do Differently*.

Sanée Bell (@SaneeBell) is the principal of Morton Ranch Junior High in Katy, TX. She has served as an administrator since 2005 at both the elementary and secondary levels. Sanée was recognized as the 2015 Katy ISD Elementary Principal of the Year. She has presented at conferences at the local, state, national, and international level, and has written publications and several guest blog posts focused on leadership and its impact on students and teachers.

Also Available from Routledge
Eye On Education
www.routledge.com/eyeoneducation

10 Perspectives on Innovation in Education
Edited by Jimmy Casas, Todd Whitaker, and Jeffrey Zoul

Essential Truths for Teachers
Danny Steele and Todd Whitaker

Your First Year: How to Survive and Thrive as a New Teacher
Todd Whitaker, Madeline Whitaker Good, and
Katherine Whitaker

Classroom Management from the Ground Up
Todd Whitaker, Madeline Whitaker Good, and
Katherine Whitaker

**What Great Teachers Do Differently, 2nd Edition:
17 Things That Matter Most**
Todd Whitaker

What Connected Educators Do Differently
Todd Whitaker, Jeffrey Zoul, and Jimmy Casas

Dealing with Difficult Parents, 2nd Edition
Todd Whitaker and Douglas J. Fiore

**Leading School Change, 2nd Edition: How to Overcome
Resistance, Increase Buy-In, and Accomplish Your Goals**
Todd Whitaker

**Teaching Matters, 2nd Edition: How to Keep Your Passion and
Thrive in Today's Classroom**
Todd Whitaker and Beth Whitaker

Education Write Now, Volume II

Top Strategies for Improving Relationships and Culture

Edited by Jeffrey Zoul and Sanée Bell

Routledge
Taylor & Francis Group

NEW YORK AND LONDON

First published 2019
by Routledge
52 Vanderbilt Avenue, New York, NY 10017

and by Routledge
2 Park Square, Milton Park, Abingdon, Oxon, OX14 4RN

Routledge is an imprint of the Taylor & Francis Group, an informa business

Library of Congress Cataloging-in-Publication Data
A catalog record for this title has been requested

ISBN: 978-0-367-02646-2 (hbk)
ISBN: 978-1-138-33897-5 (pbk)
ISBN: 978-0-429-39851-3 (ebk)

Typeset in Palatino
by Apex CoVantage, LLC

Contents

Preface

Ten education writers sat around a conference table in Chicago, eating chocolate-covered macadamia nuts (thanks, Winston!), clicking their hotel pens, and debating the topic for this year's volume of *Education Write Now*. They asked themselves, *What are the most pressing needs in education today? How can we write a book that helps our fellow teachers and school leaders make improvements in their building or classroom?*

Someone threw out the term "relationships," and everyone nodded in agreement. Building strong relationships with teachers, colleagues, administrators, and families is at the heart of what we do as educators. But is the topic "overdone" these days? A lot of people talk about the value of relationships. Is it common sense? Would it make a worthwhile theme for this book?

Jeff, Sanée, Onica, Randy, Winston, Laura, Sean, Elisabeth, Rosa, and Danny thought about it for a while. It dawned on them that while a lot of people discuss *the why*—why we need strong connections, there's not a lot on the *how*. How do you connect with students and peers in a way that truly enhances learning and culture? How do you move beyond icebreakers the first week of school to intentional, sustained effort throughout the school year?

Jeff wrote "Relationships" on the Google doc projected in the front of the room, and everyone started to flesh out their ideas. Suddenly Onica exclaimed, "Relationships Matter, People!" Of course, that soon became the theme of the writing retreat weekend, and the term RMP was tossed around during peer editing sessions, full group read alouds, and team dinners over deep-dish pizza.

We never ended up making those RMP T-shirts we joked about, but the authors really nailed it with the topic. Relationships do matter, and how we go about them daily and consistently makes all the difference.

The authors spent the three days of the retreat writing about their varied experience in this area and sharing a plethora of strategies. Each author focused on one specific aspect of relationship-building:

♦ Connecting the dots among students and staff (Jeffrey Zoul)
♦ Strengthening relationships in the learner-centered class (Randy Ziegenfuss)
♦ Building a culture of equity and access (Rosa Isiah)
♦ Cultivating student strengths and interests (Elisabeth Bostwick)
♦ Bridging the gap between schools and families (Laura Gilchrist)
♦ Deepening connections through productive conflict (Sanée Bell)
♦ Finding relationships beyond the four walls (Onica Mayers)
♦ Connecting through the power of generosity (Winston Sakurai)
♦ Bringing passion into the schoolhouse (Sean Gaillard)
♦ Tapping into dreams for a world-class culture (Danny Bauer)

The authors have served in different roles in schools throughout the country, but they've found commonalities about what it really means to recognize, celebrate, and work with individuals, and how that lays the foundation for everything we do as teachers and leaders. I'm so pleased I had the opportunity to work on their book, and I hope you find it helpful and inspiring.

I'm also pleased that I had the opportunity to work with this fabulous team—ten outstanding educators who, throughout the retreat weekend, practiced what they preached about relationships. By getting out from behind their desks, writing collaboratively, sharing ideas, respectfully disagreeing, providing feedback, and taking risks together, they not only produced great work, but they also forged bonds that will last for years to come. (And I should add that most of them hadn't met before this event!)

Now we turn it over to you, the reader. We hope the strategies give you some new ideas to try or some new ways of thinking, and we would love to hear how it goes. Please connect with us beyond the pages of this book, and continue the conversation on Twitter using the hashtag #EdWriteNow. Best of luck on your journey! And remember that no matter how tired you are and how busy life gets, Relationships Matter, People!

—Lauren Davis, Publisher, Routledge

Meet the Contributors

Jeffrey Zoul (@jeff_zoul) is a life-long teacher, learner, and leader. During Jeff's distinguished career in education he has served in a variety of roles, most recently as Assistant Superintendent for Teaching and Learning with Deerfield Public  Schools District 109 in Deerfield, Illinois. Jeff also served as a teacher and coach in the State of Georgia for many years before moving into school administration. Zoul has also taught graduate courses at the university level in the areas of assessment, research, and program evaluation. He is the author/co-author of many books, including *What Connected Educators Do Differently, Start. Right. Now. - Teach and Lead for Excellence, Improving Your School One Week at a Time,* and *Leading Professional Learning: Tools to Connect and Empower Teachers.* Zoul is president of ConnectEDD, an organization specializing in educational conferences, professional learning, consulting, and coaching. Jeff blogs at jeffreyzoul@blogspot.com.

Randy Ziegenfuss (@ziegeran) is Superintendent in the Salisbury Township School District. In addition to blogging at WorkingAtTheEdge.org, Randy co-hosts two podcasts at TLTalkRadio.org and ShiftYourParadigm.org.

Rosa Isiah (@rosaisiah) currently serves as principal in California. Her experiences include 24 years in education. Dr. Isiah holds a BA in Sociology, an MA in Educational Leadership, and an Ed.D in Educational Leadership for Social Justice. She learns and leads with passion and purpose.

Elisabeth Bostwick (@elisabostwick) is an educator who's passionate about empowering learners to identify their interests and leverage their unique strengths to shine. As a result of relentless dedication to moving education forward by creating a culture of innovation, Elisabeth is the recipient of the New York State Excellence In Teaching Award and was named the lead PBS Digital Innovator of New York in addition to the NextGen Leader in Education. She is the author of the upcoming book, *Take the L.E.A.P., Ignite a Culture of Innovation*. Elisabeth is driven to elevate education by giving back to the greater good while serving as a support and source of inspiration to others. Learn more at www.elisabethbostwick.com.

Laura Gilchrist (@LauraGilchrist4) is Champion of Collaborative School Leadership & Connected Ed/City Ecosystems to elevate youth. She is the Instructional Coach at Turner High School in Kansas City. She spent 20 beautiful years as a middle school science & social studies teacher.

Sanée Bell (@SanéeBell) is a middle school principal and adjunct professor who resides in Houston, Texas. She has experience as an elementary principal, middle and high school teacher, and basketball coach. Sanée recognizes her impact as a leader and uses her role to inspire, motivate, and empower others. Connect with Sanée through her blog saneebell.com and via Twitter.

Onica L. Mayers (@O_L_Mayers) considers herself to be a #LeadLearner. Currently serving in her sixth year of principalship, she is humbled to be recognized as the 2018 Elementary Principal of the Year in her school district. By being a connected educator, she has transformed the way teaching and learning takes shape on her campus. Most importantly, she believes that being a servant leader means that you must #BeTheModel – always. Connect with Onica on Twitter and via https://mayersminutes. blogspot.com/.

Winston Sakurai (@winstonsakurai) has distinguished himself as an innovative educational leader at the state and national level for over 25 years. He was recently recognized by the National Association of Secondary School Principals as a 2016

National Digital Principal of the Year, the Hawaii Association of Secondary School Administrators as the 2016 Hawaii State Principal of the Year. In 1996 he was named by the *Honolulu Star Bulletin* as One of Ten People Who Will Make a Difference in Hawaii's Future along with Hawaii Governor Ben Cayetano, United States Senator Mazie Hirono, and Congressman K. Mark Takai. He previously served as the Vice Chairperson of the Hawaii State Board of Education and as a voting member of the National Association of State Boards of Education. He currently moderates #PrinLeaderChat for the National Association of Secondary School Principals on Sunday nights at 9 PM EST and serves as the Principal of The Prep in Honolulu, Hawaii.

Sean Gaillard (@smgaillard) is Principal of Lexington Middle School and founder of #CelebrateMonday and #TrendthePositive. He is author of *The Pepper Effect*, and he blogs at principallinernotes.wordpress.com.

Danny "Sunshine" Bauer (@alien earbud) is the founder of Better Leaders Better Schools the #1 blog and podcast created for leaders in education. Danny loves reading and learning, laying at the nearest beach or pool, building relationships, and has a passion to beat everyone he meets playing rock, paper, scissors. If you'd like to continue the conversation through a 1-on-1 coaching call, or explore if joining the mastermind would be right for you, I invite you to reach out to me so we can turn your dreams into a reality! My email is daniel@betterleadersbetterschools.com and you can connect with me via Twitter.

1

Connecting the Dots

Jeffrey Zoul

In 2012, Seth Godin wrote a "manifesto" about education titled *Stop Stealing Dreams* (Godin, 2012) in which he posed the question, "What Is School For?" He also delivered a TED talk on the topic that has since been viewed by hundreds of thousands of people around the world. Near the end of his presentation, he makes a claim that has resonated with me ever since: We are really good at measuring how many dots students *collect*, but we teach nothing about how to *connect* those dots (Godin, 2012). Although he was making a specific point with his statement, focusing primarily on student learning while in school, I believe the analogy can be extended to represent much about the limitations of "collecting dots" in our schools versus the power of "connecting dots" in our schools. The key to success in school is connecting. In schools where students connect with their peers and their teachers, and teachers connect with parents, and the superintendent connects with principals, and school board members connect with the community, and everyone in the school is connecting what is learned there to the world outside the schoolhouse walls, everyone wins—most importantly the students we serve. A short answer to Godin's query, "What is school for?" is simply: students. The more we can do to get our students to connect to school and investing in their own learning, the more likely it is that we will fulfill our purpose of creating schools that are for students.

The Silo Mentality

In the business world, the "Silo Mentality" can be defined as the "mindset present when certain departments or sectors do not wish to share information with others in the same company. This type of mentality will reduce efficiency in the overall operation, reduce morale, and may contribute to the demise of a productive company culture" (Gleeson, 2013). A similar version of this mentality applies to school communities, including not only the adults working in the schools, but also the students learning in the schools. Too often in schools, we exist and perform in silos. It may be mere coincidence, but the word "silo" is but one letter removed from the word, "solo," and the meanings of the two words—at least connotatively—have much in common. When we work in silos, we are likely working solo, even, ironically, when we are in a classroom with thirty students or a faculty meeting with one hundred colleagues. There may be other people involved, but oftentimes, each is focusing on their own work or their own group without connecting it to the greater good. We work in isolation, we learn in isolation, we focus on checking items off our list, and we move quickly from one thing to the next. Students move from classroom to classroom or subject to subject, with little time devoted to connecting what they are learning in one area to another. Teachers spend the vast majority of their time in their own classrooms focusing on their own lessons, data, and students. Building administrators spend a majority of their time leading within their own school silo as well, while district administrators focus on their primary silo of responsibility, whether that means finances, operations, human resources, school-community relations, or curriculum. School communities in which members collect dots within silos may be good, but school communities in which members connect the dots between silos can become great and eventually break down the "silo mentality" completely. Schools that *connect*, rather than merely *collect*, dots work intentionally to create a culture in which each individual is invested not only in their own work and learning, but also how this work and learning relates to others, how it relates to the mission and vision of the classroom, school, and district, how it relates to their personal goals and dreams, and how it relates to the world beyond the schoolhouse walls.

The Things We Collect

In schools, it does seem like we focus on "collecting" quite a few "dots." Perhaps we have systems in place that compel us to do so. I cannot say with certainty all that Godin meant when he exhorted people to stop focusing on dot-collecting in schools, but for me, it made sense on a number of levels. Although the analogy may well apply to every school community subgroup, it certainly applies to students, teachers, and administrators.

Student Dot Collecting: I worry that many students today—including our students who are most adept at "playing school"—have their own worry when it comes to school. They worry about how fast they can collect their next dot and what they need do to collect it. Unfortunately, they focus on the how and what at the expense of the why. There are seemingly endless dots we place in front of students for them to collect. They move from grade to grade and then subject to subject, collecting the 1st grade dot, the middle school dot, the algebra dot, and the anti bullying dot. In specific classes, they collect the spelling test dot, the research paper dot, the project dot, and the oral presentation dot. As students move from elementary school and middle school into high school, dot collecting picks up steam. Now we have them collecting dots like crazy people, making sure they collect the ACT/SAT dot, the AP dot, the athletics dot, the service learning hours dot, the college applications dot, the clubs and activities dot, and the grade point average dot.

In a never-ending, dizzying quest to collect these and so many other school dots, they cannot possibly focus on the bigger meaning of what school is for: pursuing and fulfilling personal goals and dreams and acquiring the knowledge and skills necessary to make these goals and dreams a reality.

Teacher Dot Collecting: My fear about educational dot collecting is not limited to students. I suspect we set teachers up for dot collecting as well. I taught for nineteen years at the K–5, 6–8, and the 9–12 levels and it seemed like many of my colleagues and I were forever chasing the next professional dot. Much like the students we taught, our quest, unfortunately, was not always about quality, but about quantity, running the gamut from the ridiculous to the sublime and everything in between. For teachers, dot collecting often starts with the teacher certification process and ends at retirement, with hundreds of dots collected along the way. We collect the bulletin board dot and the committee assignment dot. We collect the professional learning dot and the graduate degree(s) dot. We collect the teacher of the week, teacher of the month, and teacher of the year dots. We collect the PTA dot, the PLC dot, and the SMART goal dot. Some teachers collect the National Board Certified Teacher dot and others collect the Gifted/Talented dot or the Advanced Placement training dot. Just as is the case with students, none of these teacher dots are necessarily bad things. They are not necessarily good things, either. Just like with students, it is not about collecting the dots, but what we do with these dots to connect to a larger purpose that matters.

Administrator Dot Collecting: Unfortunately, building and central office administrators are also not immune from dot collecting. In fact, it almost seems like an ongoing game of administrator Monopoly, with participants collecting another required dot each time they pass "Go" in order to arrive at administrative Boardwalk. It may begin by collecting the mentor dot, the department chair dot, the coach (athletic and/or instructional) dot, the leadership team dot, or the School Improvement Team dot. It most certainly requires collecting the Master's degree dot and, preferably, the Specialist's degree dot and the doctoral degree dot. We collect the student discipline dot, the teacher evaluation dot, the school safety and crisis team dot, and even the bus duty and cafeteria duty dots. We collect dots to show we work well with parents, school boards, and teacher unions. We collect the membership-in-a-civic-organization dot, the publishing dot, the present-at-a-national-conference dot, and the teach-grad-classes-at-a-university dot. Again, there is nothing wrong with any of this administrative version of dot collecting. There may not be anything right about it either, though. It depends on our why, not our what or how.

If and when students, teachers, and administrators find themselves engaged in the game of dot collecting—at the expense of authentic teaching, learning, and leading—it is typically not the fault of the individual chasing the dots, but the systems in place which encourages such pursuits. We need systems in place that promote learning and growth at all levels, including the learning and growth of teachers and administrators as well as students. However, such systems must not be so structured, prescribed, and incentive laden. We must focus on connecting what and how we learn with why we want to learn and grow.

The Need to Connect

Schools should exist to teach, inspire, and motivate not only its students, but also its teachers and administrators, connecting the skills and knowledge (dots) they acquire with an individualized and personal plan of growth. I suspect that nearly every school and school district in existence has a mission statement in place that answers the question, "Why do we exist?" Having such statements in place can be a powerful force for collective and continuous improvement. I also think that every student, teacher, and administrator in the district should have a personal mission statement describing their personal "Why?" As important as mission statements are, in truly successful schools people do not merely *have* a mission; rather, they are *on* a mission, a mission that moves beyond simple dot collecting.

Students, teachers, and administrators who not only have, but are on, a mission are invested, committed, and future focused.

They are also connected: to the school, to each other, to networks of people on social media, and to the world around them. School connection increases when those in the school believe that others in the school care about them as individuals. Students are more likely to succeed when they feel connected to school. As educators, perhaps our top priority today should be to ensure that our students feel connected to our schools. Our students follow the lead of their teachers in so many things, even when we suspect they have tuned us out. And, teachers often follow the lead of their administrators. If administrators feel they are truly connected to the school community and, especially, the teachers they lead, teachers, in turn, will feel more connected to the school. In schools where teachers feel authentically connected to the school, including their administrators and their students, students will also feel more connected to the school.

Schools in which students and staff feel connected are schools that succeed. They succeed by connecting what they are doing today to something they will do tomorrow. They aspire to something grand and connect with others who can help them achieve their goals and dreams. They connect what they are learning to what they are doing. They connect academic learning to a purpose. They connect attendance and behavior expectations to group norms and citizenship. They connect social emotional learning to lifelong learning. They connect students and staff members to other students and staff members, both within the school and schools around the world. They connect science, literature, fine arts, physical education, mathematics, and history to current world events. Educators connect with the parents whose children attend the schools—not because they see it as their duty, but because they know connecting with parents increases the likelihood that students will feel connected.

There are scores of other connections to be made in schools and an equal number of methods, strategies, and tools for making these connections. It is imperative that we focus on connections in our schools. We have all seen the data (Gallup Inc, 2013). Too many students become increasingly disengaged with school the further they trek along their Pre-K–12 journey. In truth, too many teachers and administrators also become disengaged—or, perhaps, less engaged—as they continue their career in education. We need to do a better job of connecting kids to their schools and this will only happen if we first make sure that every educator in the schoolhouse is fully connected to the school in which they serve.

The Key to Connecting

How, then, do we increase school connectedness, not only among our students, but all staff members? On the one hand, the answer to this important question is, in itself, a full-length book. On the other hand, it all begins with one simple word: relationships. As Onica Mayers often reminds us, "Relationships matter, people!" In schools where student-teacher relationships are intentionally prioritized resulting in positive, supportive, friendly, and authentic multi-way conversations between and among students and teachers, students are much more likely to feel connected to their school. Such connections grow stronger still when these same students notice (and they *do* notice) that the adults in the building have also established relationships among each other that are positive, supportive, friendly, and authentic; in other words, they see that staff members do not merely work together, but are connected to each other. They talk, laugh, share stories, eat together, visit each other's classrooms, and console one another. Conversely, when kids see the adults in the building working in isolation, rarely connecting with anyone or anything outside their own classroom or office walls, they assume that this is how school should be and follow suit. The result is, at best, compliance and, at worst, defiance. What will *not* happen is the increase in student connectedness we seek and need if our students are to reach their potential as active learners invested in their own learning.

Connecting is a contagious phenomenon. It begins when we focus on positive relationships in every area of the school, including classrooms, of course, but also in cafeterias, on playgrounds, in hallways, in car rider lines, and on school buses. There is no magic bullet to building these positive relationships, but when it happens, magic is indeed the result. Students and staff work harder, have more fun, and treat each other with more kindness. John Dickson suggests that nothing is more valuable to us and value-adding than strong and positive relationships and that knowing we are valued and cared about by those we value and care about is the true predictor of a healthy sense of self-worth (Dickson, 2011). Although building positive relationships is something that cannot be forced, it also cannot be left to chance. Successful relationships in schools are not wholly unlike any other successful relationship outside of school. I know one particular couple who have been married for over twenty-five years. They have an obvious love, respect, and passion for each other that is remarkable. They seem so connected to each other that it would be easy to assume they were just meant to be together, perfect partners for each other and people who never encounter problems in their loving relationship. In fact, nothing could be further from the truth. Although it is true that they are a very compatible husband and wife team, their marriage is not without its conflicts, complications, and challenges. But, because they love each other deeply and are committed to each other for the long haul, they long ago also committed to working on their relationship, spending time each and every day engaging in intentional acts to strengthen their relationship so that, in times of inevitable turmoil, their relationship will not only survive, but thrive. They do not take the relationship for granted; instead of simply saying many years ago, "Well, we are married now so let's agree to love each other forever," they actually focus on ways to not only maintain their love for one another but also build upon their love for one another. The love they continue to show for each other is magical, but it did not happen by magic. It happened as a result of a fierce, mutual, ongoing intention to continuously find new and better ways to connect with each other.

Obviously, there are many differences between a husband-wife relationship and teacher-to-teacher relationships or student-teacher relationships. But there are also similarities and lessons to be learned. First, it cannot be assumed. Just because you are a student in my class (or a teacher in our school) does not mean that I can expect you to like and respect me. I definitely *want* you to respect me. Honestly, I also want you to like me. But I must earn both. Moreover, once I have earned it, I cannot presume I am finished. I must continue to exhibit the behaviors that helped to make the connection, as well as finding new ways to strengthen our bond as we move forward together. A third similarity between lasting and loving romantic relationships and positive school-based relationships are two words critical to any successful relationship: Trust and Empathy. Just as in the case of successful marriages, successful schoolhouse relationships are built on the foundational pillars of trust and empathy. Students and staff members will feel more connected to the school when they trust each other. Students and staff members will also feel more connected to the school when people in the school make it a habit of seeking to understand the unique perspectives of others. Our kids (and staff members) will perform better in school when they feel connected to the school. The key to connecting students (and staff members) to school are positive relationships. The keys to building more positive relationships with our students (and colleagues) are trust and empathy.

A Connected Culture

When I was a first year assistant principal at an elementary school, a parent of a 2nd grade student came to meet with me. She was concerned about her daughter, who suddenly seemed to dread coming to school. In two previous years at the same school, this child had loved school and could not wait to race off each morning to her classroom. She was worried about her daughter and wondered why her daughter had changed. In truth, her daughter had not really changed at all. Instead, what had changed was her teacher. The teacher she had in 2nd grade was, in many ways, the polar opposite of the teachers she had previously adored, learned with, and felt connected to in both Kindergarten and 1st grade. The parent thought the change was something within her daughter, when I, unfortunately, knew the truth: the change within her daughter was merely a symptom; the root cause of the problem was a classroom teacher who was woefully inadequate when it came to connecting with her students.

In many schools, the reality is that in some classrooms (and schools) students (and staff members) feel totally connected to their teacher (leader) and school. In others, students (and staff members) who are not unlike the students (and staff members) in the other classroom (school) in every other way are significantly less connected to their teacher (leader) and school. The variable, as is often the case, is a school culture variable, not a student variable, teacher variable, or curriculum variable. Even in schools with the most toxic school culture imaginable, one still finds pockets of connectedness among staff and students. Sadly, however, such schools will never move beyond these pockets of connectedness, and the pockets will tend to be not very deep. On the other hand, in schools with positive and productive school cultures, the chances of connecting becoming contagious are greater. These schools may not be perfect and there may well be some classes led by teachers who still struggle to connect with their kids or help their kids connect what they are learning to their personal dreams and goals, but this will be the exception rather than the rule. The primary responsibility for creating school and district cultures of connectedness starts (but cannot stop) with school and district administrators. Just as the tone, mood, climate, and culture of the classroom starts with the teacher and becomes adopted by the students, the school and district cultures start with the administrator and eventually become part of the very fabric of the school, or, "the way we do things around here."

The impact of school culture upon student and staff connectedness cannot be overstated. It can be the difference between Disney World and Dismal World in terms of how engaged and invested students and staff members are in their school environment and the people with whom they interact while there. School leaders must make time to discuss the importance of school connectedness and then work with all staff members to create a culture of connectedness.

In the midst of writing this chapter on "connecting" and student and staff "connectedness" and how to create a culture—as opposed to pockets—of connectedness for the 2018 #EdWriteNow project, I decided to connect with my Personal Learning Network (PLN) on Twitter to elicit suggestions. I sent two simple Tweets to crowdsource answers to the question: How can we better connect students and staff members to school? Within a few hours, I received over forty responses. Honestly, I was not expecting much due to the space limitations of Twitter, but was pleasantly surprised by the wisdom and insights they Tweeted. Here are some tips for connecting staff and students, shared by educators around the world (I've included the Twitter handles of everyone who shared; you may want to add these educators to your Twitter PLN):

@bbbullis By giving them a voice. It could be a voice into makeup of the physical structure, the management of the classroom, or their own learning pathways. Students seeing their thoughts and ideas coming to fruition through our actions is a powerful process!

@teresagross625 I know it sounds simple, but talking to them! Making them feel cared about, loved, and that you are interested in them as a person and not just a student.

@Cmcval1930 Include them in everything you do, recognize their efforts, show them how to use Remind 101, Twitter, etc. keep communication lines open, allow them to pursue their passions, allow them to take on leadership roles, allow them to fail so they can succeed.

@Mrjonresendez By empowering them to help with big picture projects and tasks. By engaging them with leadership opportunities.

@JohnFritzky Do more than say hi. Get to know students and ask about their interests consistently throughout the year.

@MissAndersonESL Trust & support. I would walk in their office & say, "So, I have this idea . . ." and they would respond with, "yes . . . go for it." I see a lot of posts from teachers saying things like, "my admin won't let me do _____" and it makes me so thankful that I've only known support from my admin.

@Mrs_Koppers Connect to students personal lives. Make it authentic.

@teachintjay One of my best principals treated his staff respectfully and we knew we could trust him. We volunteered as a faculty continually in the community. We were happy, connected, supported, and our Students benefited from having happy teachers.

@MsFord Be visible during the day, engage in (personal & professional) small talk, listen & support ideas, carry through and support those activities which support positive student & teacher morale.

@jennteachtech Student clubs!! Such a huge opportunity for student engagement and school connectedness by giving them the space to form communities around their interests. I headed a 5th grade club around the card game *Magic the Gathering*, and it brought so many shy kids out of their shell!

@BSKUPS They will learn to trust and respect you more for being an open book tying all your lessons to something that matters outside the four walls of your classroom! Be human and kids will love you and your class for it!

@MHortonleads I run after school clubs to build positive relationships w kids: Engineering, Arduino, Electronics & Soldering, Nature Photography, Coding, Entomology, Podcasting, and drones as well as mentoring robotics teams. And I believe that it helps kids connect with school and a caring adult.

@instoessel Making myself available even when it requires giving up my lunch time with colleagues. Sometimes they need to know we care more about what they are going through, than academics.

@principalboots They don't get connected to schools, they connect to people! If the building stands empty, there is no draw. Kids want the smiles, enthusiasm, and investment that positive and engaged educators bring.

@NicholeFolkman Let them know how happy you are that they are there. Notice and praise great things they're doing. Support their amazing ideas. You need to be connected and happy to be there, too. It goes a long way. Be a listener. I never feel less valued than when I feel unheard.

Copy/ paste my answer to the question about making staff feel connected, too. People want love and respect— that includes our students and staff members.

@ellendamore Kids need to know how they belong. This requires finding common interests and appreciation in differences. They need time and support to build a positive self image, relationships, group dynamics, and empathy. Then they will feel a sense of belonging.

@CauleyMr It's the simple things: saying hello to them in the morning or in the hallway. Making sure that in that moment you are telling them that they are important, they matter. Not just with words, but with your full attention. When you celebrate those light up shoes, mean it!

@Blocht574 Show up at their extra curricular activities, write them letters and notes . . . Model the connection.

@Shogey13 Dare to be an open book. Be funny, but with expectations. Tie your lessons into real-life experience. They will look forward to being in your classroom, and maybe even feel like they can't miss it.

@AngieMChurch Sponsor a club that is created by student interest and offer support to students who are interested, then empower kids to make the club what they want it to be.

@melodystacy We put a priority on empowering our entire staff as leaders.

@wykeshahayes Rotate breakfast chats with your students in manageable-size groups once a week to allow open and honest dialogue.

@EffectualEdu Give them ownership of meaningful projects with significant impacts. Let them see you do little things that show you're invested—pick up trash in the yard, clean little messes, check up on people who were ill or struggling. Create ways to get honest feedback and do something with it.

@jen37982447 I try and show my students that I am human. I am a person just like them. This enables them to let their guard down and connect.

@SputlockLaramie Have fun! Go outside and play at recess, shoot hoops, jump rope, joke and let them know you care. As a principal, I play as much as I can.

@DrPaulKish1 Encouraging staff to learn from each other. I created "Sharing Good Practice" where a teacher presents a unique teaching idea, activity, resource, etc. that is likely beneficial for others. This activity also starts each department chair meeting. Their ideas/strengths matter.

@Mschroeder6 Two-way communication is the key to building relationships. Give them voice, choice, & leadership opportunities.

@theladyparkpark Make school a part of a student's playground. I weave social media, pop culture, music, popular characters, etc. into my classroom.

@sandeeteach 1. Connecting kids to peers—globally via Skype, etc. 2. Student blogs 3. Genius hour 4. Global read-aloud, Global play day, etc. 4. The Arts 5. Library/Media Centers, especially for younger kids who can't use social media (Edmodo, Canvas, etc.) to communicate outside of school hours 6. TIME to read books of choice.

@Andrea_Trudeau Make it fun and make spaces student centered! My "no-ssh" library has music playing, board games to enjoy, a makerspace, squishy tiles on the floor, student art on display. We say hello to all who enter and make small talk to get to know all students. Little things go a LONG way!

@curriculumblog 1. Give teachers a platform 2. Multiply leaders 3. Teacher voice/Decision-making 4. Team building and off-campus activities 5. Invest in teachers 6. Create a culture of risk-taking 7. Celebrate people and wins.

@GenoJennifer Providing some level of autonomy in their work builds trust and increases morale. We all dislike things being done to us, so intentionally finding ways where teachers are empowered to take the lead. Once this becomes your culture, the possibilities are endless!

@KimGriesbach Connection also comes from building a family atmosphere—celebrating the positives and happy moments/events, supporting each other during the difficult times, checking in on each other, etc.

What Versus *How* and *Why*

When we suspect that students are disconnecting from us, or school in general, it may behoove us to reflect on the extent to which we are prioritizing *what* we are teaching and *what* they are learning over *how* and *why* we are teaching and *how* and *why* our students are learning. The why is a particularly powerful starting point. Why do we teach? Why would students want to learn? I suspect the answer to why we teach has changed and must continue to change. The purpose of teaching can no longer be primarily to transfer information to students. In most instances, they can gain this knowledge more effectively and more efficiently elsewhere. Administrators must become lead learners and facilitators of learning within districts and schools; teachers must become lead learners and facilitators of learning within classrooms. There will always be a need for teachers to identify learning standards that must be met and teach a certain amount of basic concepts and skills, but we can—and should—be spending less time on this and more time inspiring students to make connections between what they must learn, how they choose to learn, and why the learning matters at all in their lives.

As important as it is to reflect on the question regarding why we teach, it may be even more important to ponder the question about why students want/should want to learn. In schools today, some might argue that the first answer that comes to mind is, "because they have to." Yet, even to the extent that this answer might represent the perspective of some students in some schools, it would only apply to what they are learning when they are actually in school. All students (and all human beings) want to learn. We are hardwired to live as learning, dynamic, evolving people. Even our most reluctant learners in our schools are active learners when outside the school walls. Perhaps they seek to learn about baseball, computers, gaming, rap music, or the stock market. Or perhaps they want to learn how to repair a motorcycle, ride a horse, skateboard, or create a podcast. Whatever the knowledge or skills, all students want to learn. What they want to learn and how they want to learn may deviate from our prescribed notions of what and how they should learn, but their "Why?" remains. They are motivated to learn for a number of reasons, including their interests, passions, and current skill set. A key to building strong relationships with anyone is—as mentioned previously—empathy. Now more than ever, educators must see learning from the student point of view, including determining why they want to learn and using that information to determine what and how to teach. I will never argue for allowing students to indiscriminately do what-ever they want in schools, but I would argue that we can take what and how they want to learn and why they want to learn it into account when we are planning instruction. If we make the time to consider student perspectives when examining state standards and planning lessons, more often than not we will find that student "Whys?" can easily be aligned to current state standards. Once we realize this, we can then begin designing learning experiences that are aligned to state standards *and* to each student's motivation to learn.

What we teach matters. It matters a lot. It should be aligned to learning standards. Yet, our standards allow for a great deal of autonomy, which, in turn, provides us the autonomy to include the student perspective when determining our what. Although it will always be appropriate to focus on what we teach, perhaps we first need to focus on why we teach and how we teach, reminding ourselves along the way why and how our students want to learn. When we take into account how and why our students learn, and only then determine what they will learn with our guidance, we are more likely to connect our kids to us, the content, their own learning, their future goals, and our schools. A final note about *How and Why first; then What*: When working to create a connected school culture, it is almost always the case that what we need to do for our students, we also need to do for ourselves. Adults, like students, are more motivated to learn, perform at higher levels, and connect with the school community when school leaders remember to focus on adult "hows" and "whys" before dictating any school or district "whats."

Reimagining Dots

In its current form, dot collecting on the part of students, teachers, and administrators in our schools is counterproductive to authentic learning and optimal performance. But perhaps we need only reimagine the concept, transforming dot collecting into a motivating and genuine part of the learning process. An unfortunate outcome of status quo dot collecting is the idea that school becomes a race, a race that many students and staff enter only to finish. Even winning is not necessary in these kinds of races; finishing is all that matters. In schools at which students and staff are truly committed to each other and truly committed to designing and participating in authentic learning experiences, students and staff wake up each day racing *to school* as opposed to *racing away* from school at the end of each day, the end of each school year, and, ultimately, at the finish line, whether that finish line is graduation (students) or retirement (staff).

How, then, do we authentically connect students, teachers, and administrators to the schools in which they learn, teach, and lead? Maybe it begins by reimagining dots and reimagining education's version of racing. The key to reimagining dot collecting lies in turning over control regarding what dots to collect from the teachers, administrators, school boards, and politicians who currently assign them to the students, teachers, and staff currently collecting them. The more we can focus on why we want to teach, learn, and lead, allowing the dot collector to become—at a minimum—a co-designer of the actual dot, including how and what they will teach, learn, and lead in order to earn the dot, the more likely it is that we will connect them to our schools and invest them in their own learning, teaching, and leading.

The problem with status quo dot collecting in schools is that we are asking other people to collect *our* dots, not *their* dots. We need to shift our thinking, focusing on the person collecting the dots, the person running the race. For fifteen years, every 4th of July I ran the Peachtree Road Race in Atlanta. It is the world's largest 10K road race with over 60,000 runners taking part each year. With a race of that size, the race director and other organizers play extremely important roles. It is not a stretch, in fact, to say that certain components of the planning process are matters of life and death. It is an experience that must be carefully designed every step of the way. This team of planners is extremely important; the race could not go on without them. At the same time, the race is not about the race director, nor her team members. Instead, it is about the runners who run the race—60,000 unique individuals with 60,000 different running styles, paces, goals, reasons for running, race day routines, racing strategies, and training plans. The 60,000 runners even get a voice in the final Peachtree Road Race ultimate dot: the coveted finisher's T-shirt. Prior to the race itself, participants get to vote for their favorite T-shirt design from among several choices.

Much like the Peachtree Road Race staff members, educators play extremely important roles in the lives of their students and each other. In fact, some of our decisions are also literal life or death decisions to some of the people we serve. We must design races for students and staff that have them focused not only on the finish line, but also on the present, racing to school each day to get what they need and what they want in order to keep growing and learning as opposed to getting what we think they need merely to finish. Several years ago, my friend and colleague Marcie Faust, and I were working together in the Teaching and Learning department at a school district in Illinois. We worked on a project together, trying to answer the question, "How can we get our students to run to school each day?" As part of our work, we decided that students and staff need to run a new kind of school race, one that focuses much more on each individual running the race and much less on the race directors or the race course. We even created an acronym to capture key components of a race we believed would make more students and staff run to, not away from, school each day. Schools that succeed in connecting students and staff to their schools and to each other focus on creating a **R**elevant, **A**ctive, **C**urious **E**nvironment in every classroom and throughout the school. When we create school and classroom **environments** that include **relevant** and **active** learning experiences and that arouse **curiosity** within the students, teachers, and administrators working in these environments, we are not only collecting more authentic dots in more personalized races, but also connecting those dots to meaningful goals and dreams. Let's reimagine the race that education has become, doing everything in our power to ensure that races to nowhere become races of possibilities to anywhere.

References

Dickson, J. P. (2011). *Humilitas: A lost key to life, love, and leadership.* Grand Rapids, MI: Zondervan.

Gallup, Inc. (2013). 'The School Cliff: Student Engagement Drops With Each School Year.' Retrieved from https://news.gallup.com/opinion/gallup/170525/school-cliff-student-engagement-drops-school-year.aspx.

Gleeson, B. (2013). 'The Silo Mentality: How To Break Down The Barriers.' Retrieved from www.forbes.com/sites/brentgleeson/2013/10/02/the-silo-mentality-how-to-break-down-the-barriers/#1e8bb2d18c7e.

Godin, S. (2012). *Stop Stealing Dreams: (what is school for?).* Seth Godin at TEDxYouth@BFS. Retrieved from www.youtube.com/watch?v=sXpbONjV1Jc.

2

Relationships

The Foundation in Learner-Centered Environments

Randy Ziegenfuss

I cannot teach students well if I do not know them well.

Ted Sizer

What do we believe about powerful learning? What does it mean to build meaningful relationships with learners, family, peers, qualified adults, and community members in a powerful learning environment?

These questions have been the focus of our work in the Salisbury Township School District for the past several years as we work to transform our schools from a traditional school-centered environment to an ecosystem that is learner-centered, promoting learning of the most powerful kind. As we have engaged in transformation work, the relationship question has frequently surfaced as we learn that relationships in a learner-centered environment are different from school-centered.

But before we get to the *Why, What* and *How* of relationships in a learner-centered environment, I want to be clear on what makes learner-centered different from school-centered as they are two very different paradigms we use to think and talk about education.

Two Different Paradigms

School-centered education is the dominant conversation that happens in our schools today. This conversation is filled with beliefs and values such as:

- Learning happens in schools.
- Education is done to the learner.
- Learners are known by how they compare to their class averages on standardized tests.
- Learners must be compelled to perform.
- The system focuses on having the most effective teaching.
- The learner adapts to the standardized system.
- Effectiveness is achieved through standardization.
- All learners follow standard paths at standard paces and demonstrate mastery in standardized ways.
- Educators teach to the average learner and manage exceptions as problems (Education Reimagined, 2015).

While school-centered is presently the dominant conversation around education, there is a growing number of pioneer educators who believe that school-centered beliefs and values do not lead to the most powerful learning opportunities. Instead, they believe that through a paradigm shift, powerful changes in learning can happen in schools – changes that authentically place the learner at the center.

- Learning happens in learners.
- Education is done by (and with) the learner.
- Learners are known as individuals – each with their own unique strengths, interests, and goals.
- Learners want to learn.
- The system focuses on having the most effective learning.

- The system adapts to the unique learner.
- Effectiveness is achieved through customization.
- Each learner moves on their own path at an appropriate and adaptable pace.
- Every learner is exceptional. The uniqueness of learners is not a problem but, instead, something to build on (Education Reimagined, 2015).

Education Reimagined calls this a paradigm shift and presents this in their visioning document:

> The learner-centered paradigm for learning functions like a pair of lenses that offers a new way to look at, think about, talk about, and act on education. It constitutes a shift of perspective that places every learner at its center, structures the system to build appropriate supports around him or her, and acknowledges the need to adapt and alter to meet the needs of all children.
>
> The learner-centered paradigm changes our very view of learners themselves. Learners are seen and known as wondrous, curious individuals with vast capabilities and limitless potential. This paradigm recognizes that learning is a lifelong pursuit and that our natural excitement and eagerness to discover and learn should be fostered throughout our lives, particularly in our earliest years. Thus, in this paradigm, learners are active participants in their learning as they gradually become owners of it, and learning itself is seen as an engaging and exciting process. Each child's interests, passions, dreams, skills, and needs shape his or her learning experience and drive the commitments and actions of the adults and communities supporting him or her.
>
> (Education Reimagined, 2015, p. 5)

If, after reading, you are more curious and intrigued about learner-centered education, visit Education Reimagined at http://education-reimagined.org.

Context: Our Path to Learner-Centered

One more thing before we get to relationships in a learner-centered environment . . . a little bit about our path to learner-centered in Salisbury . . .

The work of transformation in the district has truly been a collaborative effort. All stakeholders in our small Pennsylvania community – school board, leadership team, teachers, learners and community – have had the opportunity to enroll in this work, but I want to highlight our Assistant Superintendent, Lynn Fuini-Hetten, as a key collaborator and leader of this work. What I describe here is undeniably *our* work. Transformation of this kind has to be collaborative . . . it is not sustainable if it is the work of one or even a few.

In 2015, we crossed paths with a white paper published by Education Reimagined that helped transform our thinking about learner-centered education, *A Transformational Vision for Education in the U.S.* (http://bit.ly/EdWriteNow-01). The language in the document outlines a "North Star" of five elements of powerful learning environments and became the core of conversations in Salisbury about powerful learning experiences for our learners. Powerful Learning is:

- ◆ Competency-based
- ◆ Personalized, relevant and contextualized
- ◆ Characterized by learner agency
- ◆ Open-walled
- ◆ Socially-embedded

Shortly after being introduced to learner-centered education, we began engaging in conversations with stakeholders focusing on two questions:

- ◆ What knowledge, skills and dispositions do our learners need for success after graduation?
- ◆ What learning environments do we need to create to support the development of those sets of knowledge, skills and dispositions?

As a result of this year-long work, we adopted a Portrait of a Graduate and beliefs about learning. (Visit http://bit.ly/salisbury-POG.) Then came the heaving lifting of actually transforming a system and working with our stakeholders to shift mindsets from school-centered to learner-centered.

It's been a challenging process. A time intensive process – a process that is far from complete. Throughout the work many curiosities and inquiries have developed. One of those has been around leadership and what kinds of new sets of knowledge, skills and dispositions we need as leaders to lead this transformative work.

With that inquiry in mind, Lynn and I committed to our own action research project focused on two questions:

- ◆ What knowledge, skills and dispositions do leaders need to lead learner-centered environments?
- ◆ What distinguishes learner-centered leadership from traditional school-centered leadership?

To engage in this inquiry, Lynn and I decided there was no better way to learn the answers to these questions than to speak with leaders and learners in learner-centered environments across the country. That's exactly what we did. In May of 2017, we launched the Shift Your Paradigm podcast (http://shiftyourparadigm.org) and have been engaging in rich conversations to deepen our own understanding of learner-centered education and learner-centered leadership.

So how does *relationship* fit in with this work? After over 40 conversations, it became clear to us that relationships are at the core of learner-centered environments and that learner-centered relationships look different from relationships in the dominant paradigm, the school-centered paradigm. Thus emerged new curiosities:

1. Why are relationships key in learner-centered environments?
2. What distinguishes relationships in learner-centered environments?
3. How do we cultivate deep relationships with learners and others in learner-centered environments?

Finally, a bit of a disclaimer: This is work in progress. The *why*, *what* and *how* are based on conversations we have had with learner-centered leaders and learners. As we continue to learn ourselves, we will undoubtedly deepen our thinking about learner-centered education and the role of relationships. Think about the ideas shared here and how they may fit into your current context, regardless of where you are on the school-centered/ learner-centered continuum.

The work of transformation is characterized by iteration and experimentation, so I hope you will give some of these ideas about relationships in a learner-centered environment a try, reflect on your implementation and create the next iteration of the idea to move your school or district closer to the vision for learner-centered education. I'd also encourage you to share your work – accomplishments and failures – with the wider education community. It is only through your sharing that the learner-centered movement will become the dominant conversation of today and tomorrow.

Let's talk relationships!

Why are Relationships Key in Learner-Centered Environments?

Look no further than the *socially-embedded* element as outlined in the Education Reimagined whitepaper, *A Transformational Vision for Education in the U.S.* (Education Reimagined, 2015, p. 7.):

> Socially-embedded learning is rooted in meaningful relationships with family, peers, qualified adults, and community members and is grounded in community and social interaction. It values face-to-face contact, as well as opportunities to connect virtually, and recognizes the significance of establishing continuity in children's lives through the development of stable relationships. Independent exploration and practice; collaborative group work; structured, intentional instruction; and structured and cooperative play, among other experiences, are integrated to develop learners' competencies. Both peers and adults are recognized as integral partners in

learning, and learners are encouraged to interact with those developing at different competency rates, from different backgrounds, and with different interests. Furthermore, socially embedded learning catalyzes and structures partnerships with families, community-based employers, civic organizations, and other entities that can foster learning.

Social interaction and relationship building is an integral part of all powerful, deep learning. Plain and simple. Take away connection between learner and others and you have a limited or nearly barren learning environment – certainly not one that we would consider learner-centered. At the macro level, relationships can happen in both face-to-face and virtual environments with learners of any age and background including peers and adults. Learners can also build and engage in relationships that extend beyond the classroom walls. This is known as open-walled learning.

Relationships are at the center of the work in a learner-centered environments. For example, learners may be collaborating (co-laboring) to design a solution for a water run-off challenge in a local community park. In this scenario, learners collaborate and in the process strengthen their relationships with each other as well as others outside the school connected to solving the challenge – engineers, the local environmental council, the community organization providing funding and other relevant stakeholders.

In contrast, a common example of an experience void of human relationship would be learners engaging in test prep in front of a computer. While limited learning (knowledge building and skill development through repetition and memorization at a low cognitive level), the learning is transactional and devoid of any human relationship, interaction or connectivity. It is certainly not learner-centered since the learner is not at the center. The school system and its need for quantitative accountability are placed in higher regard than the learner in this scenario. Powerful learner-centered environments always involve human relationships with others.

Neuroscience can also help us understand the important connection between relationships and learning. In Kirke Olson's book, *The Invisible Classroom: Relationships, Neuroscience and Mindfulness in Schools*, he reminds us of the biochemical dance that occurs when people connect. Oxytocin levels increase as personal stories, life details, passions, challenges and dreams are shared (Olson, 2014, pp. 137–138). Elevated oxytocin levels lead to increased trust and the ability to determine trustworthiness, an increased feeling of connectedness and a reduction in stress levels.

The culture in today's school-centered learning environments contains system structures that reduce time for relationship and connection: over-emphasis on standardized tests that measure academic growth in a narrow set of content areas, curriculum content that is broad and shallow, pedagogy that relies on teachers imparting information to passive recipients. These processes focus on the left hemisphere of the brain and lower the value of right-brained connection and the triggering of oxytocin. Connection and relationship are biological imperatives for satisfying the social brain and release space for the left brain to build knowledge and skill sets.

What Distinguishes Relationships in Learner-Centered Environments?

Now that we've established the connection between learner-centered education and relationships, let's examine what distinguishes relationships in a learner-centered environment. In this section, we'll look at five characteristics of relationships in a learner-centered environment based on conversations that have been part of the *Shift Your Paradigm* podcast series. Keep in mind that this list has been generated based on a limited data set along with my own practice as an educational leader.

Relationships in Learner-Centered Environments Focus on Learning – Academic, Social/Emotional and Personal

In the current dominant paradigm of school-centered education, how often do conversations move beyond the transactional and into the realm of understanding each other as learners? This is a significant question when attempting to understand the difference between relationships in school-centered environments and learner-centered environments. It's moving beyond more than just "How was your weekend?" Or "How is your sister?" Conversations are intentional, focused on learning and lead to deeper understanding of teacher and learner.

Andrew Frishman, Co-Executive Director of Big Picture Learning (BPL) shared how BPL has redefined the 3 Rs.

> . . . that it should be about our relationship, relevance, and rigor. You start with relationships and get to know people. That's how you figure out what young people are interested in and that's how you get to that really deep rigor. If you braid those three of relationship, learning through interest, and practice together, that's how you get to these really deep, powerful learner-centered opportunities that really ultimately shift life outcomes and trajectories.
>
> (Fuini-Hetten, et al., *Episode 15*)

It's relationship that ties relevance and rigor to the individual. Knowing the person adds to the personalized approach of relevance and rigor. These words are not about curriculum or standards, but the person. If they were, relevance and rigor would be viewed through the school-centered paradigm. Because they are tied to relationship and the person, relevance and rigor are seen through the learner-centered paradigm.

A key vehicle for building deep relationships in BPL schools is the advisory program. Naseem Haamid, a learner at Fannie Lou Hammer Freedom High School at the time of our conversation, shared how the relationship between himself and his advisor begins with a focus on learning:

> She puts me in a position to succeed rather than fail. So, if she knows I'm interested in politics, she'll connect me with the local elected official, right? And get me an internship and get me an interview where I'm able to be

in a position where I'm able to succeed and learn more about myself and grow. And every time an opportunity comes across her desk, and it's something that I might be interested in, she'll reach out to me.

(Fuini-Hetten, et al., *Episode 15*)

"Learning" includes the academic as well as the personal and social/emotional aspects of getting to know learners. These conversations extend into learning not valued by traditional assessment such as balancing priorities, and life outside of the classroom and at home. Naseem once again:

Or if I have a problem, like, this year was a very stressful year for me since it was my senior year, whether it was applying for college or doing an event with student government, I could always go to my advisor and speak to her about what leadership means. And my teacher, I look at her as a leader, you know, she broke everything down for me and told me that I needed to delegate my responsibilities and put other people in positions where they can do great work along with me. So, I would say that's my experience. And inside the classroom it's not only either. I feel like it's universal with all teachers since in my building all teachers are advisors. They understand the students' needs and they know that what's going on isn't only inside the – inside the classroom or inside the school building. You might be going through things at home and you may need assistance, and advisors are always there to help out.

(Fuini-Hetten, et al., *Episode 15*)

Naseem later added: "But you have to take time to understand a student as a whole. Not only how they learn, but their emotions" (Fuini-Hetten, et al., *Episode 15*).

Ezekial Fugate, Head of School at Springhouse Community School in Floyd, VA also speaks of the multiple facets of relationship beyond academics to include personal and social/ emotional learning:

For us, relationship is really central to everything that we do and that's relationship to self, so having an understanding of who am I, what are my gifts, what's getting in the way, what brings me alive, what puts me asleep? So relationship to self, relationship to other, how do we actually show up in a world where there are people that we might not like? Maybe people that we really like, but how do we do the hard work of attending to human relationships and so we spend a lot of time in relationship in the community really cultivating the skills to navigate challenge, to navigate tension, to navigate any sort of issue that arises.

(Fuini-Hetten, et al., *Episode 23*)

In addition to relationships being grounded in conversations around dimensions of learning, these conversations grow deep roots over time and can often last for years once learners leave the learning environment.

Relationships in Learner-Centered Environments are Deep

In *Episode 25*, we had an extended conversation about relationships with Andrew Frishman and Carlos Moreno, Co-Executive Directors of BPL. Andrew recalls a speaker he saw once that prompted him to think about the deeper aspects of conversations and relationship building in contrast to the "small talk" that often occurs in America.

I heard a speaker, his name is Gilberto Dimenstein, and he talks about the importance of learning in community and situated learning in learning cities. He's from Brazil, and he was talking about one of the cultural differences he sees in the United States. People have this small talk before they then get on to the important business talk, and he said, "You know, where I come from there is no small talk." That's the important talk. The important talk is connecting us to human beings. I think we have a bit of that view [at BPL] as well that the relationship building, the connection, the understanding where you're coming from, who your family is, your communities, your experiences, what your goals and aspirations are. That's not small talk. That's the important talk. That's what enables and, you know, you go slow a little bit at the beginning to build those relationships so that you can go really fast together.

(Fuini-Hetten, et al., *Episode 25*)

Carlos added a "niece-nephew analogy" that sheds light on how deep and meaningful conversations and relationships can be around learning and the "important talk."

I wanted to share really an analogy that one of our colleagues has used in describing what this relationship really means and he has labeled it as his "niece-nephew analogy." Really consider thinking about, if you don't have a niece or nephew, you can substitute any young person you cared deeply about who's not your own child. How do you talk to this person individually on a one-on-one? How do you inquire into their interests if approached by them with an exciting idea, something they're eager to do or investigate? How do you respond to that? How might you help them learn about something they express interest in? Would you try to share your own learning with them, and how was your caring about the world manifest in your interactions with this young person? Really thinking – applying this analogy in teacher practice really means thinking of your advisory as a collection of these young people you get to interact with at the same time. And I think that's the primary reason why a lot of our students really refer to their advisory as kind of their – their second family.

(Fuini-Hetten, et al., *Episode 25*)

Learner-centered relationships run deep. They are not transactional and as Carlos and Andrew share later in the interview, they often continue after learners leave the BPL learning environment. Notice Carlos' question, "Would you try to share your own learning with them . . .?" This leads into the next principal of learner-centered relationships uncovered in our conversations.

Relationships in Learner-Centered Environments are Multi-Directional

Another theme that has emerged from our conversations is that relationships are built in both directions. You can already see this in some fields outside of education, such as the medical field, where a model known as reverse mentoring fosters broader collaboration and a greater agency and voice on the part of learners (Meehan, 2018). In a school-centered paradigm, relationships tend to be uneven – more teacher questioning and learner sharing; less collaboration between the two. Learners may be sharing personal information about themselves to teachers, much of which is rarely used to design learning opportunities, while the teacher less frequently shares their experiences as a learner.

Naseem from BPL described the learner-centered alternative at BPL. "So, like, you learn – in a Big Picture Learning school, you learn from the teacher and the teacher learns from you and you both grow together. And that's the – that's the beauty of it" (Fuini-Hetten, et al., *Episode 15*).

At Springhouse, adults model two-way relationships with each other in ways they hope they will engage learners in relationship building conversations. "We really don't look at our learners as coming in as sort of empty buckets that we need to fill up. We really try to acknowledge what they bring to the table. I think that we as the community of adults in the school really practice what we're trying to teach. So we actually take a lot of time to tend to our relationships and to make sure that we're doing everything that we're asking our students to do. I'd say there's a lot of integrity in what we're doing" (Fuini-Hetten, et al., *Episode 26*).

Such openness and vulnerability creates a culture of trust and listening in learning environments such as in Alamo Heights Unified School District in Texas (Fuini-Hetten, et al., *Episode 3*). Clara Lew Smith, a learner from Vermont working with UP for

Learning, spoke to the importance of listening and trust in the learner/teacher relationship as well:

> I think that the basis for that [invitation to be heard] has to be an understanding relationship and one built on trust. I think that students who really trust that adults want to hear what they have to have say, and they're willing to listen to their feedback, and willing to use it to actually make change, are more willing to accept that invitation.
>
> (Fuini-Hetten, et al., *Episode 30*)

When caring adults and learners are sharing equally, an interesting dynamic occurs regarding power and control that doesn't exist in typical school-centered learning environments.

Relationships in Learner-Centered Environments Transfer Power and Control

There's a flattening of hierarchy. The teacher's expertise no longer dominates. Each brings an expertise to the conversation and the relationship. The teacher, a content and learning design experience; the learner, a personal experience around a passion, need, challenge or dream. These are equally honored in the process of building relationships in learner-centered environments. Power and control are shared. This shift invites and values agency on both sides of the relationship.

Elizabeth Cardine, lead teacher and advisor at MC² Charter School in New Hampshire was eager to bring the role of power to light in our conversation in *Episode 19*:

> I think something that a lot of stakeholders, students, parents, and the teachers themselves have to constantly be on guard against because it's so ingrained in the status quo of teacher is this idea of where does the authority come from in the teacher-student relationship and the role of power and the role of hierarchy and experience.
>
> (Fuini-Hetten, et al., *Episode 19*)

Kim Carter, CEO at MC² extends what Elizabeth shared and refers to learners and how they learn to "manage up":

> We are encouraging students to manage up. And that's so different from what traditionally happens in an adult-youth relationship. And some of the research suggests that can be very challenging, very threatening for an adult to have a younger person managing up to them. So building the structures around the expectations for how that works, I think, is an important thing.
>
> (Fuini-Hetten, et al., *Episode 19*)

This kind of transfer of power to learners and their voice requires vulnerability on the part of teachers. Jenny Finn, Dean of Students at Springhouse:

> I think that [valuing vulnerability] is something that is foundational here. We recognize that connection – authentic, true connection – cannot happen without vulnerability. And so we definitely move toward vulnerability and not away from it. And like Ezekiel said, this does take time and energy. And I would also say it takes skill.
>
> And so we are – whatever we're teaching and doing – we're pretty much holding that at the forefront. What are the skills that these students need to be more resilient in the world, to be able to really face and move through difficulty and not avoid or kind of force themselves through it but find a way that is authentic to them to really navigate difficulty in relationships in themselves or each other or the earth? And so that – having that value of vulnerability and knowing that in order for connection to happen, vulnerability needs to be there. It's important that we also teach the skills to be able to navigate that.
>
> (Fuini-Hetten, et al., *Episode 26*)

Helen Beattie, the founder and Executive Director of UP for Learning summarizes the flattening of hierarchy and distribution of agency in the learner-teacher relationship that is one of the principals of learner-centered relationships:

> I think one critical piece of this shift of paradigm and the relationship of students and teachers goes right to the heart of power. And who has power? Right now, in our traditional system, certainly, it's largely held by adults. And a learner-centered paradigm requires a sharing of power, that both are empowered within the relationship. And I think for so many adults, that is a frightening concept and it feels antithetical to where they need to go. They've always believed that power is how they get to this destination.
>
> (Fuini-Hetten, et al., *Episode 30*)

While most relationships in education are learner to teacher, it's important for the relationship building to extend beyond the walls and into the larger learning community as more learning environments embrace the element of open-walled learning.

Relationships in Learner-Centered Environments Extend Beyond the School and Into the Community

This idea of building relationships with community partners comes through in the work of One Stone, an independent, student-led high school in Idaho. Chad Carlson, Director at One Stone provides a glimpse into how these relationships look and are built:

> And that's really what I think we do at One Stone and I think we do a – it's something – our forte is our reliance and our relationship with community partners. And so, a big part of the design lab is thanks to community members who were willing to embrace and work with high school students, giving them voice, and having trust in what they can do. A lot of what they do in design lab, there's a lot of research involved. There's a lot of writing

and proposals and rationales and their case studies that they do. So, there are a lot of things that you could achieve through these kind of ideas of state standards or that you get in common core that they get through this experience.

I think the big difference is that they're bought in and they have a relationship with the community partner that they feel a lot more accountable and they feel like that they're held accountable to this either organization or individual. And so, there's more buy-in from the student. So, I think that kind of helps I guess overcome these barriers or obstacles is really just embracing what is out there.

(Fuini-Hetten, et al., *Episode 29*)

As learner-centered environments become characterized more by learners solving challenges in the community, building relationships with outside partners becomes more important. The value of community partnerships is not unique to One Stone. Iowa BIG has an instructional model that is almost entirely project based with very few actual courses (Fuini-Hetten, et al., *Episode 5*). Learners work on community challenges with teachers backmapping learning to content standards. BPL schools with it's "Learning Through Internships" emphasis asks learners to make personal connections with community regarding their passion and interests. These initial connections eventually lead to job shadowing opportunities and internships (Fuini-Hetten, et al., *Episode 15*).

How Do We Cultivate Deep Relationships with Learners and Others in Learner-Centered Environments?

I hope that your interest in learner-centered education, particularly the aspect of relationships in these environments has been piqued! Now what? We must take action. It's time for us to put what we know about relationships in learner-centered environments into action. Here are a few ideas to get started.

Build the Mindset for Learner-Centered Education
and Relationships in Learner-Centered Environments
in Yourself and Others

The more that Lynn and I do this work in our district, the more we remind ourselves of the word "mindset." To lead an organization toward learner-centered education and an understanding of relationships in that environment, we really must begin with ourselves, building our own understanding so that we are able to enroll others in this new way of thinking about education. Some of my favorite resources about learner-centered education are housed on these sites:

- ◆ Education Reimagined: http://education-reimagined. org
- ◆ Shift Your Paradigm podcast: http://shiftyourparadigm. org
- ◆ Students at the Center: https://studentsatthecenterhub. org
- ◆ CompetencyWorks: www.competencyworks.org

Once you've deepened your own understanding, the next step is to build the mindset in others. As educators, we can't force our new learning and a new paradigm on others (that would be very school-centered!) but rather, we need to *enroll* those in our organizations into new ways of thinking about learning and relationships and an understanding of the *Why* shared earlier in the chapter.

Enrollment. Probably not a word that you would associate with shifting mindsets, but it's actually a very effective (and learner-centered!) tool for engaging others in the process of shifting mindsets. We learned this process from Allan Cohen during an Education Reimagined Pioneer Lab Training.

So what is enrollment? Enrollment *is not* about arguing. It's not about selling. And it's not about getting somebody to do something. It *is* about creating the conditions for someone to "see" something different through inquiry and listening. As Allan shared, "You're trying to put something in the lenses they are using to see the current situation." In this case, the current situation is the context of education and the role that relationships play. Allan shared two approaches to help us alter the "lens" so as to enroll others in a new way of thinking:

With an interested person:

- Ask/listen – *What are your concerns about . . .?*
- Invite imagination – *What would it be like for you if . . .? What would it be like for your child/that learner if. . . .?*
- Share – *What got me committed to this way of educating/ thinking is . . .*
- Share – *What I can be counted on for is . . .*
- Request – *Would you like to get more involved? One way you can support this in our community/school is . . .*

With a skeptical person:

- Ask/listen – *How do you see things? What are your concerns? What is it that I'm not understanding about your point of view?*
- Share – *What got me committed to this way of educating/ thinking about relationships is . . .*
- Share – *What I see to be possible is . . .*
- Agree, and . . . – *I agree. That is a real challenge and it is worth tackling . . .*
- Invite imagination – *What would it be like for you if . . .? What would it be like for your child/that learner if . . .?*
- Return to your stand – *I am committed to . . . You can count on me to . . .*
- Request – *Would you be willing to . . .?*

The protocols are powerful and very learner-centered. Remember, it's not about forcing the paradigm or new way of thinking on someone else – we all know that kind of leading isn't sustainable. It's about mirroring what we want to see happen in the classroom – creating conditions whereby others come to their own understanding of a complex concept or idea.

Make Time and Space for Deep Conversations and Deep Relationship Building

Shifting mindsets takes time. It requires conversations led by inquiry and filled with listening from everyone involved. Our current school-centered model does not easily allot much discretionary time for conversations and relationship building. If it's all about "relationships, relationships, relationships," then we all must prioritize our time to allow for the rich conversations that distinguish learner-centered relationship building. Many of the leaders we've spoken to have carved out time and space for relationship building by designing advisory/mentoring systems.

Establish an Advisory/Mentoring System in Your School

An advisory/mentoring program not only provides the space and time for deep relationship-building conversations, but these programs also provide the opportunity for teachers and learners to develop the skill sets necessary, to practice moving the conversations beyond transactional, personal information and into deeper areas focused on academic and social/emotional learning. The result is a deeper understanding of learners and greater ability to co-design powerful learning opportunities that are personal and relevant.

This description of the BPL advisory by Andrew Frishman paints a picture of what an effective advisory program might look like, and how it can be the space that provides for deep relationships between young and adult learners:

> It's a way to really connect with the student in – that goes beyond, far beyond just particular academic content or a specific technical skill. An advisory is way beyond homeroom on steroids, right? It's a group of 15 to 25 students who stay with one adviser over the course of two to four years. Really getting to know the students through the course of their high school experience, gives you a sense of the arc of where they're coming from, where they're going to, how they're growing and maturing.
>
> It's through the combination of deep individual relationship and getting to know the students in a

group in an advisory that allows advisers to work with students to help them lock into their interests and their passions and go out and explore. The main role of the adviser working with that student is to say, "How would you go out, if you're interested in architecture, or you're interested in early childhood education, or you're interested in culinary, how would you find some of the five to ten places in your local community where that kind of work is going on? And how could you set up an informational interview? How could you go out and do some research on the top restaurants in your area, or the top architecture firms, or the top early childhood centers?" And go in and learn to do the right kind of research ahead of time, you'll ask good questions. Everything from who are the people that work there, to how did they get their careers, to what is a day to day job – a good day to day at work look like and feel like.

And so, the role of the adviser then is to support and scaffold the student's experience out in the world of that internship. Think about what the authentic products and projects are going to be and then help with assessment of that.

(Fuini-Hetten, et al., *Episode 25*)

An advisory/mentoring program will not only support connection between learners and teachers, but may also lead to our last idea for getting started.

Begin Cultivating Relationships Outside the School and with the Community and Community Partners

Learner-centered education requires deep relationships, but we cannot do this work alone in the confines of the four walls of the classroom or school. We need to engage community partners and build those relationships that will support the dreams and learning goals of all learners in the organization.

Schools such as Big Picture Learning, Iowa BIG and One Stone realize that this is work that educators cannot do alone.

We need the community and we and our younger learners need to reach out and build relationships with people outside the organization as well.

Conclusion

I've always loved these words from Education Reimagined:

> "Learners are seen and known as wondrous, curious individuals with vast capabilities and limitless potential."
> (Education Reimagined, 2015, p. 5)

They keep me grounded and always thinking about putting learners first, both young and old. In the end, the quality of the relationships we build is dependent on the lens through which we choose to view relationship building – the school-centered lens or the learner-centered lens. Depending on which we use, the relationships will look and feel different. With the school-centered lens, relationships will be transactional, constrained by time and confined to the walls of the classroom or school.

With the learner-centered lens, relationships will always begin with the learner, focusing on conversations that deepen our understanding of people as learners, are multi-directional and diminish the hierarchy found in traditional teacher-learner relationships. Relationships in a learner-centered environment are less *knowing about people* and more about using our understanding of the academic, personal and social/emotional passions, interests and needs of others to *learn with them* and co-design the most powerful environments needed to realize dreams and goals.

How will you take the next steps to create the space for building the deep, lasting relationships today's learners need?

References

Education Reimagined. (2015). *A transformational vision for education in the U.S.* Retrieved from: https://education-reimagined.org/wp-content/uploads/2018/06/A-transformational-vision-for-education-in-the-U.S.-Logo-Updated.pdf.

Fuini-Hetten, L. & Ziegenfuss, R. (Producers). (2017, May 23). *Shift Your Paradigm – Episode 003 – Alamo Heights Independent School District Interview with Dr. Kevin Brown and Dr. Frank Alfaro.* [Audio podcast]. Retrieved from http://shiftyourparadigm.org/episode-003-alamo-heights-independent-school-district-interview-with-dr-kevin-brown-and-dr-frank-alfaro.

Fuini-Hetten, L. & Ziegenfuss, R. (Producers). (2017, June 3). *Shift Your Paradigm – Episode 005 – Iowa BIG Interview with Dr. Trace Pickering, Shawn Cornally and Jemar Lee.* [Audio podcast]. Retrieved from http://shiftyourparadigm.org/episode-005-iowa-big-interview-with-dr-trace-pickering-shawn-cornally-and-jemar-lee.

Fuini-Hetten, L. & Ziegenfuss, R. (Producers). (2017, October 10). *Shift Your Paradigm – Episode 015 – Big Picture Learning Interview with Dr. Andrew Frishman, Naseem Haamid and Terrence Freeman.* [Audio podcast]. Retrieved from http://shiftyourparadigm.org/episode-015-big-picture-learning-interview-with-dr-andrew-frishman-naseem-haamid-and-terrence-freeman.

Fuini-Hetten, L. & Ziegenfuss, R. (Producers). (2017, December 2). *Shift Your Paradigm – Episode 019 – MC2 Charter School Interview with Kim Carter, Elizabeth Cardine, Sabrina Gatlin.* [Audio podcast]. Retrieved from http://shiftyourparadigm.org/episode-019-mc2-charter-school-interview-with-kim-carter-elizabeth-cardine-sabrina-gatlin.

Fuini-Hetten, L. & Ziegenfuss, R. (Producers). (2018, January 30). *Shift Your Paradigm – Episode 023 – Springhouse Community School Interview with Ezekiel Fugate and Jenny Finn.* [Audio podcast]. Retrieved from http://shiftyourparadigm.org/episode-023-springhouse-community-school-interview-with-ezekiel-fugate-and-jenny-finn.

Fuini-Hetten, L. & Ziegenfuss, R. (Producers). (2018, February 27). *Shift Your Paradigm – Episode 025 – Big Picture Learning Interview with Dr. Andrew Frishman and Carlos Moreno.* [Audio podcast]. Retrieved from http://shiftyourparadigm.org/episode-025-big-picture-learning-interview-with-dr-andrew-frishman-and-carlos-moreno.

Fuini-Hetten, L. & Ziegenfuss, R. (Producers). (2018, March 13). *Shift Your Paradigm – Episode 026 – Springhouse Community School Interview with Ezekiel Fugate and Jenny Finn, Co-Founders; Gabby Howard and Leah Pierce, Learners.* [Audio podcast]. Retrieved from http://shiftyourparadigm.org/episode-026-springhouse-community-school-interview-with-ezekiel-fugate-and-jenny-finn-co-founders-gabby-howard-and-leah-pierce-learners.

Fuini-Hetten, L. & Ziegenfuss, R. (Producers). (2018, April 24). *Shift Your Paradigm – Episode 029 – One Stone Interview with Chad Carlson and Chloe French.* [Audio podcast]. Retrieved from http://shiftyourparadigm.org/episode-029-one-stone-interview-with-chad-carlson-and-chloe-french.

Fuini-Hetten, L. & Ziegenfuss, R. (Producers). (2018, May 8). *Shift Your Paradigm – Episode 030 – UP for Learning Interview with Helen Beattie and Clara Lew Smith.* [Audio podcast]. Retrieved from http://shiftyourparadigm.org/episode-030-up-for-learning-interview-with-helen-beattie-and-clara-lew-smith

Meehan, K.O. (2018). "How to mentor millennials in medicine: Bridging the intergenerational impasse." *Medscape.* Retrieved from: www.medscape.com/viewarticle/898797_1

Olson, K. (2014). *The Invisible Classroom: Relationships, Neuroscience and Mindfulness in Schools.* New York: W.W. Norton & Company.

Sizer, T. (1999). "No two are alike." *Educational Leadership, 57(1).* Retrieved from: www.ascd.org/publications/educational-leadership/sept99/vol57/num01/No-Two-Are-Quite-Alike.aspx.

3

Connecting with Every Student

Creating a Culture of Equity and Access

Rosa Isiah

Meaningful connections and strong relationships are the foundation for learning. When students feel that we understand who they are and that we authentically care, they take emotional risks and they open their hearts and minds to connecting and learning. Relationships matter.

As a teacher, my most important mission was to develop a deeply trusting connection with every student in my classroom. I didn't always meet my goal, but I poured my heart and soul into trying. Connecting with students, understanding who they are and the gifts that make them special, continues to be paramount to my work as a school administrator. Over the course of my 24 years in education, I have witnessed the power of connections transform the lives of students AND teachers. We all have stories to share about students who taught us incredible life lessons about learning, resilience and empathy. We also have stories about students who found their voice when they connected with a teacher who believed in them. Those transformational connections are fostered through authentic relationships. They are powerful.

Throughout my 24 years I have also witnessed a troubling pattern. I've observed that we are not always willing to give *some* students the same opportunities to connect that we may afford others. Marginalized students – students of color, socio-economically disadvantaged youth, English learners, and especially trauma impacted students – are sometimes perceived as "high-need" and "difficult" to understand and connect with. I speak from personal experience and I know that I'm not alone. Educators care about students and many dedicate their lives to teaching, but something is missing if we are leaving some of our most vulnerable students behind. How can this be, if after all, it is our moral imperative to positively influence, nurture, guide and empower our students? Are we lacking the *will* to connect with marginalized students or are we lacking the *skills* to do the heart work?

Connections and relationships are the key to establishing a culture of equity and access for all in our educational settings. When we fail to provide equitable learning opportunities and emotionally invest in some of our students, the message to those left behind is that they are not worthy of our time and our efforts. It will be impossible to close achievement gaps and develop a culture of equity and access if we do not invest the time to forge relationships and develop strong connections with our students, even when it's difficult. ESPECIALLY when it's difficult. It is our moral imperative to do better for every-single-student with whom we are privileged to work.

What's Your Why?

When I think about creating a culture of equity and access in our schools, I think about the factors that impact student learning. There are many systemic failures across the country that impact our students and are beyond our immediate control. Those systemic issues result in a need to support and enrich the schooling experiences of our students. At times the task feels bigger than we can handle, but remember that WE ARE the system and we have the power to begin the change we need to see in our schools.

Teaching is incredibly rewarding and at times a highly demanding responsibility. We are literally saving lives when we connect with students and empower them with the skills to overcome adversity and live their best lives. It is easy to become overwhelmed with the *what* of our work, the test scores and teaching and learning gaps, but let's get back to the foundational and most critical aspect of our work in education. The *why*. The reason we became educators, the love of learning and joy that we feel when students learn. Let's not lose sight of the *why* along our educational teaching and learning journey.

The *why* in my work as an educational leader is equity and access for all students. Inequity and oppression in education are the topics that keep me and many of us up at night. The great news is that we can create changes in education that tackle inequity and oppression, and those changes begin through our relationships with the people we serve. Sir Ken Robinson said it best, "You are the system and you can change education." Indeed, and we can achieve that through the power of relationships. We become strong advocates *for* children when we build strong relationships *with* children.

Why Does Connecting with Every Student Matter?

Connecting with every student matters because every student matters. At the end of the day, an educator's goal is learning for students and a desire to increase student achievement. We want students to have access to quality education in an engaging, caring and safe environment, but when learners are distressed or feeling disconnected, learning does not take place. Unfortunately, the data indicate that too many students are not accessing this type of learning, connection, or learning environment. Understanding who our students are is the best way to begin creating the ideal and necessary conditions for learning.

This is why connections and relationships with every student matter:

- ◆ Children who grow up in poverty have higher risks of mental health issues as adults.
- ◆ Children growing up in poverty have low executive function. "Regular exposure to these stresses in

childhood can inhibit early development of the neural connections that enable executive function, leaving children with both academic and behavioral problems" via www.scilearn.com/blog/ten-facts-about-how-poverty-impacts-education.

◆ Traumatic experiences (Adverse Childhood Experiences ACEs) and chronic high levels of stress negatively impact and alter a child's brain, resulting in difficulty paying attention, learning, and even aggression (Adams, Caposey, & Isiah, 2018).

◆ Although the U.S. Dept. of Education estimates that 4.5 million English learners are enrolled in public schools across the U.S., bilingualism is discouraged across the nation. Bilingualism is perceived by some to be un-American (Mitchell, 2016).

◆ High School dropouts are 63 times more likely to be incarcerated (DuFour, DuFour, Eaker, & Many, 2006).

◆ Average test scores of black students are on average two grade levels lower than those of white students in the same district; the hispanic-white difference is roughly one-and-a-half grade levels (Rabinovitz, 2016)

◆ African American citizens are twice as likely to be poor compared to white citizens (Muhammad, 2018).

◆ Students with disabilities are twice as likely to be suspended from school as those without disabilities (Muhammad, 2018).

◆ Latinos continue to lag other groups when it comes to earning a bachelor's degree. In 2012, 14.5% of Latinos ages 25 and older had earned one. By contrast, 51% of Asians, 34.5% of whites and 21.2% of blacks had earned a bachelor's degree (Caumont, 2013).

The data clearly indicate that we have achievement and opportunity gaps in our schools. As noted, many students, especially historically marginalized students, students of color, trauma-impacted students and students living in poverty, are not all learning at high levels nor making sufficient academic gains to prepare them for a 21st-century world.

Many of the students in our classrooms and school communities are represented in the data points mentioned. Change for our students is possible. Change begins with a belief in their ability to learn and a culture of connections and strong relationships in schools. I have personally witnessed the power of connection and access in a healthy and equitable learning environment and its impact on an entire school community. Meet my former student, Michael . . .

Connecting with Michael

Michael was a new student to our school who came to us with a number of concerns. He was a student that was pushed out of his former school district for what many would identify as aggressive, inappropriate and defiant behavior. He enrolled in our school district the prior year and attended a different school. He was struggling in every academic area and was "at-risk" of retention. His mother was labeled contentious and unsupportive in the school community. She defended Michael's behaviors without question and Michael knew this. As a new student to our school district, Michael quickly figured out what he needed to do to avoid the school environment.

Michael acted out.
Michael's mother showed up to school and defended his behaviors without question.
Michael was rewarded with the opportunity to go home with a referral or school suspension.

After months of this behavior, Michael was facing expulsion and his mom chose to disenroll him from the district and enroll at a private school. He attended that school for about 6 months and was asked to leave as a result of his behavior. The principal and staff at his home-school were concerned about his return and Michael was recommended for enrollment at my school site with the intention of giving him a "fresh start." My school community is small and word got around that Michael would be enrolling. Teachers were concerned about getting this new student and I found myself having the same concerns. I caught myself and shamefully admitted to my team that I, too, was overwhelmed with concern and doubt about Michael's behaviors and the impact he would have on his peers and teacher. The impact on our school. What was I thinking? Michael was a student who clearly needed second, third and fourth chances. I realized that we had the opportunity to change Michael's schooling experience and trajectory in life. We decided to embrace him and do exactly what we preached that we and others should do for students.

We arranged to meet with Michael's parent prior to enrollment to set up a plan for support and success. We gathered our school-wide support team that included a counselor, classroom teacher, nurse and teacher learning specialists. We talked about our school, our expectations for all students, and we encouraged his mom to share her expectations of us and for her son. Michael's mom felt that he had not been treated fairly in the past and that teachers didn't care about him, but was glad to be at our school. I explained to her that we had the same goal, we wanted Michael to succeed. I told her that we were caring and fair, and lovingly firm when needed. I ensured her that we all wanted him to be the best student that he could be. We also offered additional check-ins and academic intervention supports. At the end of the meeting it was clear that we were all on the same page and ready to move forward with a new chapter for Michael.

The following week Michael came in with the perception that his experience would be the same. He worked at making his presence known and introduced himself as the new "bully" of the school. Our school does not foster a culture of bully behavior and students and teachers were diligent about letting him know that those behaviors were unacceptable. Michael followed up with a few more unbecoming attempts to establish himself as the schoolyard bully. He was disrespectful to adults and students, did not like to share and picked on younger students. Our school team continued to discuss ways to support Michael. His teacher was firm and caring. She promoted structure and accountability. She connected with him and the things he loved to do. She discovered that Michael was creative and enjoyed making things. She tapped into those gifts and gave him opportunities to share his talents with others. I met with him and checked in with him frequently, often to simply say hello. I made sure that every adult at school knew who he was, not as a warning, but because I understood how important it was for him to feel connected, accepted and part of our school community. Teachers and staff befriended him and welcomed him to the school "family." I'm proud to share that with the support and connections with staff and students, Michael had the best year of his academic career. He worked through challenges and mistakes when he made them. He made impressive academic gains with the supports he received from his teacher and our specialists. He understood that we expected great things from him and that no one would give up on him. Michael formed relationships with his teacher and staff, and he felt connected to his new school community. Michael ended the year on a strong note.

Michael also taught US a great deal about ourselves that year. He reminded all of us how important relationships are to learning.

- ◆ We learned that connections and authentic relationships HEAL.
- ◆ We were reminded of the power of relationships.
- ◆ We were reminded that we all deserve second (and third and fourth) chances.
- ◆ We were reminded that every student, especially our most vulnerable students, deserve a safe and trusting learning environment that promotes a culture of equity and success for all.

There are many students in our schools at this very moment that are in desperate need of connection and acting out in ways that command your attention, positive or negative, and the attention of their peers. If behavior is communication, what are those students communicating to you and how might you begin to support them in a different way? Who is your Michael and what are you prepared to do to learn more about him? What will you do to educate his heart and mind and change his life?

What Does It Mean To Create A Relationship-Driven Culture of Equity and Access?

Many would say that connecting with children is a natural part of our work as educators of young minds. It's what the majority of educators desire to do because we know how POWERFUL connections are for students . . . connections to self, connections to text, connections to other people. We can reference research that indicates the importance of connections and how those connections lead to learning at high levels. We understand its significance, but really . . . can we truly say that we're connecting with *every* student in our classrooms? In our schools? The truth is that we are not and we can always do better. As noted in the previous section, data on the current achievement and opportunity gaps for specific groups of students support the need for connections and demand a call to action. Here are a few tips to help you create a relationship-driven culture of equity and access in your classrooms and in your schools.

Begin the Change by Looking in the Mirror: Implicit and Explicit Bias

The strategies that can be used to create a culture of deep connections and a culture of equity and access in the classroom begin with you. Change begins by acknowledging that our beliefs and practices contribute to the problems that many children and educators face in education. Everyone has biases, implicit or explicit, that impact how we interact with our students and peers.

Implicit bias is defined by the Ohio University Kirvan Institute for the Study of Race and Ethnicity as the attitudes or stereotypes that affect our understandings, actions and decisions. The biases can be positive or negative and can be initiated unconsciously and involuntarily. Most people are unaware that they are expressing implicit bias. This is why it is so important to create a space where data is analyzed and educators can have honest and courageous conversations about how they contribute to the achievement and opportunity gaps.

Explicit bias is defined as the attitudes, beliefs and behaviors that one has at the conscious level. Hate speech, negative stereotypes, racist rhetoric and discrimination against certain groups is explicit bias. Explicit bias is not only conscious, but also intentional and controllable. Unfortunately, there are people in education who have explicit biases as a result of fears or ignorance. I strongly believe that we do not have the time or place in our schools for anyone who is explicitly biased. We should not accept or tolerate it, especially in today's political climate where some, including people in power, are attempting to normalize this type of negative and deliberate hurtful rhetoric.

Biases of any kind, implicit or explicit, are barriers to learning for many of our students. Take a moment to look in the mirror and ask yourself the following questions. They will help you determine your biases and how to change them:

- ◆ What are your biases about certain groups of students?
- ◆ Do you believe that every student, regardless of race, gender, or socioeconomic status, can learn at high levels?
- ◆ Do you treat female and male students differently? Do they have similar opportunities to learn?
- ◆ How do you seat or call on students?
- ◆ Do you value your students' home language and culture? Do you see language and culture as a hindrance or an asset?
- ◆ Who are the students in your classroom that you feel the most comfortable connecting with?
- ◆ Are you taking the time to build strong connections with every student in your class or school?
- ◆ Who are you sending to the office with an office referral? Same students? Students of color?
- ◆ Are you analyzing data and noticing achievement gaps for English learners, Students of color? Students impacted by poverty?

- Does your school have an over-representation of suspended or expelled subgroup of students?
- Do you have an over representation of Students of Color or ELs in your Special Education programs?

Connecting with Students: Developing the Skills

A 2015 study, Who Believes in Me: The Effect of Student-Teacher Demographic Match on Teacher Expectations, by the Upjohn Institute shares the following: ". . . what's important to know about implicit biases is that, once people are made aware of them, those biases can be successfully addressed. We can mitigate them. We can interrupt them. You can train your mind to catch yourself." It's like breaking a habit, but the first thing you have to do is become aware of the habit. This is not about blaming or demonizing teacher behaviors. This is about developing awareness and changing behaviors. Every one of us has biases. The great news is that we can make changes. Once we better understand more about our biases, beliefs and connections with students, we can make changes that will foster deep relationships and help develop a positive learning community where all students have the opportunity to learn at high levels. Here are a few recommendations:

- Get to know your students: Take time to understand who they are and where they come from. Find out what they are interested in learning.
- Work closely with your professional learning team. Analyze data and look for gaps and patterns. Ask yourself and answer the following questions:
  - How will we know if our students feel connected and supported?
  - What is it we want our students to learn?
  - How will we know if each student has learned it?
  - How will we respond when some students do not learn it?
  - How can we extend and enrich the learning for students who have demonstrated proficiency? (DuFour, DuFour, Eaker, & Many, 2006).

- Families are a big part of the relationships we have with our students. If you want to know who your students are, make an effort to establish connections with their families.
  - Do not make the assumption that parents don't care if they are unable to show up for parent conferences or school events. Some parents have to choose between working to feed their kids or taking a day off to attend a school event.
  - Do not make the assumption that students in poverty are unloved or neglected by their families. A lack of resources is not commensurate with neglect.
- Language and culture matter. Don't be afraid to ask questions about a student's home language and culture. When you ask questions and learn about a student, you validate who they are.
- Believe in a student's ability to learn.
- Model a growth mindset and teach students how to develop it. Errors should be celebrated sources of learning.
- When working with marginalized or disadvantaged students our job as educators is NOT to save them from their lived experiences. Instead:
  - Acknowledge their experiences.
  - Focus on providing engaging learning opportunities.
  - Help students develop their own voice.
- All students deserve rigor and high expectations.
- Believe in your students with your whole heart.
- Acknowledge and celebrate diversity. Diversity makes us stronger.
- And most important . . . become a Culturally Responsive Teacher.

Culturally Responsive Educators Foster Relationships with Students

Jacqueline Jordan Irvine and Willis D. Hawley conducted an overview of research on Culturally Responsive Pedagogy in 2011 titled *Culturally Responsive Pedagogy: An Overview of Research on Student Outcomes* (2011) for the organization

Teaching Tolerance, a great resource and organization. Their research highlighted 6 very important "pedagogical influences on student learning" and the top influencer was *developing caring relationships with students while maintaining high standards.* Irvine and Hawley determined that a common finding of research on student learning was the importance of positive teacher-student relationships that focused on teachers' building relationships that result in positive academic consequences for students. They also shared the following about the importance and characteristics of a Culturally Responsive Teacher:

> Culturally responsive teachers understand that students bring their culturally influenced cognition, behavior, and dispositions with them to school. These teachers not only understand student differences related to race, ethnicity, culture and language, but they use this knowledge to enrich their teaching in ways that enhance learning opportunities. Achievement relevant student assets, according to Hurley, Allen, and Boykin (2009), include students' interests and preferences; motivational inclinations; passions and commitments; prior experiences and knowledge; existent and emergent understandings and skills; personal, family and cultural values; family traditions and practices; attitudes, beliefs, and opinions; self-perceptions; and personal or collective ideologies.

All of the tips mentioned will help you develop the skills needed to strengthen your relationships with students. The first step is identifying your personal beliefs about students and how your behaviors impact your ability to make deeper connections with ALL students. Overcoming biases is not an easy process but understanding that they exist, that you have biases as we all do, is the first step toward becoming a Culturally Responsive Educator who possesses a sense of urgency about creating a culture of relationships, equity and access for all.

Who Does the Work?

John Hattie speaks about the influence of the classroom teacher on student achievement. "It is teachers who have created positive teacher student relationships that are more likely to have the above average effects on student achievement" (Meteor Education, 2018). Based on his *Visible Learning: A Synthesis of over 800 Meta-Analyses relating to Achievement* work (Hattie, 2009), one of the most impactful indicators on student achievement is the teacher-student relationship. The teacher-student relationship had an effect size of 0.72. Anything over .40 is meaningful and impactful. In other words, the relationship that educators have with their students dictates the level of impact that educators will have on a student's overall achievement. WE HAVE THE MOST IMPACT WHEN WE DO THE WORK. We should constantly ask ourselves what type of impact we want to have on our students.

Teachers are the most influential people in a student's school life. Their influence has tremendous impact, but it truly takes a village to change the lives of children. School administrators, staff, parents and other students are the soul of the school. The entire team of stakeholders makes up the culture of a school community. Culture is identified as the norms, values, beliefs and behaviors of the organization. All together, we have the power to create and sustain the culture and the climate of a school. The culture can be positive or negative. Students and staff THRIVE in a positive culture where relationships are priority and all have high expectations for learning. In *Revisiting Professional Learning Communities at Work* (2008), Rick DuFour and Robert Eaker share that "in order for a school to be a place that provides high levels of learning for ALL students regardless of student background, the staff must articulate through their behaviors that ALL children *can* learn and that all children *will* learn because of what WE do."

Yes, we all play a part and have the responsibility of creating and maintaining a healthy learning environment and culture for our students. The work of making deep connections begins with understanding who we are and what we believe about our students. Analyzing our biases and their impact on our relationships with children and staff is a great way to launch the work. Looking in the mirror, asking difficult questions of ourselves and following up with action when we don't like what we see is key. Our students, all students, deserve sincere connections. We know that when they connect deeply, they feel safe, supported, and they learn at high levels. It is my wish that every educator will make relationships with students a priority in their journey to learning, leading, and creating a culture of equity and access for all.

How Did I Get Here? Relationships, Relationships, Relationships

I remember the surreal feeling of walking across the graduation stage three years ago to receive my doctoral degree in Educational Leadership for Social Justice. I shook the dean's hand as he congratulated me and I looked up at my family waving and smiling. It was an unbelievably proud moment and the highlight of my academic career. I remember feeling exhausted and emotional, and wondering how in the world I'd gotten there.

My journey is similar to the journey of many of our students. My path was blessed with the love and connections of teachers who changed my life's trajectory. That journey began as a young four-year-old who was brought to America from another country in search of education and better opportunities for the entire family. Looking back it was the relationships with educators that fueled my love of learning and encouraged me to dream bigger than I believed possible. I refused to live a life of poverty. I refused to be like some of my friends who dropped out of high school to have babies and raise families. I loved learning and I wanted more for my future. I *knew* I could have more because my teachers told me I would.

My story of connections begins with Mrs. DeLaPena. Mrs. DeLaPena was my first grade teacher. I was a newcomer to this country and did not yet speak English. Being a newcomer was frightening and my kindergarten memories are limited. Prior to my relationship with Mrs. DeLaPena I felt confused and completely lost as a young student. Late in the first grade, Mrs. DeLaPena organized an after school club and she taught us to read and write in Spanish, my home language. Mrs. DeLaPena was the first educator who valued my culture and my language and made me feel visible. She gave me the confidence to take risks as a learner and a reader of both English and Spanish. My fondest school memories begin with my experiences in Mrs. DeLaPena's class.

Mrs. DeLaPena was not the only one who made me feel like a brilliant learner. In the sixth grade Mrs. Scotty, our instructional aide, hugged me at graduation and handed me a special note: "Congratulations, Rosa. I can't wait to read about you in the papers someday." Mrs. Scotty worked with us throughout the year and truly cared about students. I'm sure she didn't realize how much I cared for her and how inspiring that note was for me. After receiving her note I decided to write down my life's plan that evening. My list, in no particular order, included the following goals:

- ◆ Become a teacher and a principal someday.
- ◆ Publish a book.
- ◆ Marry a nice man and have a great family.

Thanks to Mrs. Scotty I have achieved all three of my sixth grade life's goals.

My middle school years were tougher. Sadly, I can't say I made deep connections with any of my teachers. I've never taught middle school but I imagine that it is a challenging transition for many students. It's a tremendous time of change. I wish my teachers knew how much I needed them to connect with me during those years.

In high school I was an outgoing scholar and part of our school's Student Leadership team. Mrs. Clear was our Leadership class teacher and our school's assistant principal. She was also an outstanding role model. She was a bilingual Latina educator who mentored many of us. Although I was a great student with college bound credits and promise, I never really believed I could go to college until I connected with her. Months before graduation she shared her college student journey and story with me. Mrs. Clear's story was so similar to my story as a young Latina growing up in poverty. She was a first generation college student who grew up in our neighborhood and faced similar challenges. She wasn't expected to attend college but persevered and did. Mrs. Clear and I connected on a deeper level after that day and she convinced me that I, too, could be a college grad.

My relationships with Mrs. DeLaPena, Mrs. Scotty and Mrs. Clear are a strong part of why I am doing the work I am so fortunate to do today. My teachers took the time to build relationships with me and they challenged and supported me when I needed it. I'm here BECAUSE of my relationships with teachers. I would not be in a position to share and learn with you without their love and support. I am grateful and I want to do the same for many, many, more students.

Connections and relationships are the key to establishing a culture of equity and access for every student in our schools. We can close achievement and opportunity gaps when we invest and connect with EVERY student. Relationships matter and every student deserves a school full of caring adults who are willing to do everything in their power to help them achieve. Relationships mattered to me as a young scholar and they will matter to the many students that you will connect with. Let's change lives.

Every child deserves a champion — an adult who will never give up on them, who understands the power of connection and insists that they become the best that they can possibly be.
Rita Pierson

References

Adams, J., Caposey, P.J., & Isiah, R. (2018). *#FULLYCHARGED: 140 Battery charging Maslow and Bloom strategies for students, parents, and staff.* Monterey: Healthy Living.

Caumont, A. (2013). *13 data milestones for 2013.* Pew Research Center. Retrieved from www.pewresearch.org/fact-tank/2013/12/23/13-data-milestones-for-2013/.

DuFour, R., DuFour, R., Eaker, R., & Many, T. (2006). *Learning by doing; A handbook for professional learning communities at work.* Bloomington: Solution Tree Press.

DuFour, R., DuFour, R., & Eaker, R. (2008). *Revisiting professional learning communities at work: New insights for improving schools.* Bloomington: Solution Tree Press.

Hattie, J. (2009). *Visible learning: A synthesis of over 800 meta-analyses relating to achievement.* New York: Routledge.

Irvine, J. & Hawley, W. (2011). *Culturally responsive pedagogy: An overview of research on student outcomes.* Retrieved from https://secure.edweek.org/media/crt_research.pdf.

Meteor Education (2018). *What does research tell us about the importance of teacher-student relationships.* Retrieved from https://meteoreducation.com/teacher-student-relationships/.

Mitchell, C. (2016). Bilingual education poised for a comeback in California schools. *Education Week.* Retrieved from www.edweek.org/ew/articles/2016/10/12/bilingual-education-poised-for-a-comeback-in.html.

Muhammad, A. (2018). *Transforming school culture: How to overcome staff division.* Bloomington: Solution Tree Press.

Rabinovitz, J. (2016). Local education inequities across U.S. revealed in new Stanford data set. *Stanford News.* Retrieved from https://news.stanford.edu/2016/04/29/local-education-inequities-across-u-s-revealed-new-stanford-data-set/.

4

Connecting with Learners

The Power Behind Cultivating Strengths and Interests

Elisabeth Bostwick

Enthralled in a fall festival design challenge, learners in my room were abuzz with excitement as they designed prototypes of their idea. Immersed in the role as fall festival designers, learners were tasked with the objective to consider what attractions and games should be offered to appeal to their peers. Enthusiastic about our school's upcoming fall festival, the challenge was highly relevant. While the purpose was to spark curiosity, engage, and spring-board collaborative communication through team building, what resulted remains with me to this day and continues to influence my thinking and every decision I make as an educator.

I stood in awe, observing how naturally students interacted with one another. Their communications took me by surprise as this was a new group of learners, many of whom were unfamiliar with one another. Students were respectfully speaking and listening to their peers, then sharing insights in return pertaining to their challenge. With a promising outlook for the school year ahead, I suddenly overheard a student, Logan, exuberantly exclaim, "this is the *best* school year ever!"

Just as I was about to pat myself on the back for an auspicious start to the school year, Abby, Logan's teammate, gave him a side glance and responded swiftly with a contemptuous tone, "You do know that once the first few days of school are over, it'll never be like this. We'll go right back to how we've always learned in school, and it'll be boring. Get over it."

Ouch. Hearing Abby's comment stung; it felt a little harsh given the palpable synergy felt amongst our room. Fortunately, Logan avidly continued working on his fall festival project design, unphased by Abby's response. As for me, I knew I had to get to the root of Abby's comment. It was crucial that I identified ways to help her connect the dots on how learning can be joyous through cultivating and identifying strengths and interests. After all, if learners lack enthusiasm for learning what might be at risk?

In Tune with Learners

As educators, we need to be reflective and decipher what our learners are communicating through their comments, tones, and body language. Recognizing what students are expressing provides insights that inform us of how we can best approach them at that moment in addition to ways we can best support them in their learning journey. That day I seized the opportunity to unpack Abby's statement, along with the manner in which she spoke, to better grasp her perspective on school and gauge how I could help.

Based on Abby's statement, what's glaringly obvious is that her past experiences in school have caused her to develop negative feelings associated with learning in school. She viewed school as something she *had* to do rather than something she *wanted* to do. But what really struck me was that at the mere age of ten, Abby had caught on to the predictable pattern which her past teachers had followed routinely throughout the years and therefore anticipated the same this school year as well. To be honest, I admire the fact that she recognized this pattern as it demonstrated her ability to be highly observant and even analytical. Notice how we can perceive comments from learners as negative, or we can take a moment and contemplate the strengths in addition to the needs associated with it. It's all about being in tune with our learners and responsive rather than forcing them into our precreated mold.

Troublemakers and Rebels or Clever Thinkers and Innovators?

Frankly speaking, Abby is a sharp, witty, and perceptive child who looked for every waking opportunity to challenge others, even her teachers. Let's face it, students who challenge educators are often deemed to be troublemakers, rebels, or labeled as behavior problems. Truth be told, Abby's past teachers had already approached me to warn that while Abby was bright and highly creative, she had a strong tendency to be cynical and frequently bucked the system as she danced to the beat of her own drum. However, it was clear from their comments that Abby was viewed in a negative light due to her natural tendencies and unwillingness to comply with the norm, as she favored creating her own distinct ways to express her learning. For example, Abby created brilliant methods to decipher solutions to math problems and demonstrated immense creativity through writing.

Imagine a world in which all students are seen for their potential; bright, highly creative, analytical, and then encouraged to challenge paradigms of the status quo through thinking differently within their individuality and uniqueness. Imagine that! And yet, some view this as something to keep your eye on.

Although on the surface Abby appeared to be excelling academically, she maintained an extremely negative perception of learning in school due to the expectation to remain compliant; within a box of preset guidelines from years previous. Choosing to focus on the negative aspects as opposed to the positive traits of our learners will likely influence our interactions with them, even in the most subtle ways. We may be communicating unintended messages that shape our relationships, creating negative results and that's a risk we cannot afford to take.

Abby's story resonates with me because to some degree it mirrors that of my own children, Julian and Nolan. When my sons were in their younger years, they were eager to learn about everything around them. In fact, their curiosity seemed to be insatiable. The older they became, their initiative to learn seemed to diminish. We can all attest that this shift in children occurs throughout various developmental stages, but as their mother and an educator, it's concerning that they lack the motivation to learn. Or, do they?

After all, they aren't uninterested in learning at home. Both boys will devote hours to mastering whatever it is that they're focused on learning connected to their strengths and interests.

According to the 2016 Gallup report, an unsettling trend reveals that as learners go through school, engagement decreases. We can all attest to the fact that learning becomes increasingly difficult the older our learners become, but engagement is not only necessary, but critical for deeper learning to occur.

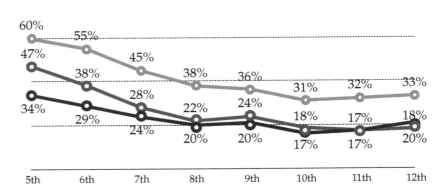

Percentage of Students Who Strongly Agree, By Grade (n = 928,888)

◇ In the last 7 days, I have learned something interesting at school
◇ I have fun at school
◇ At this school, I get to do what I do best every day

FIGURE 4.1 Gallup Report, www.longviewoneducation.org.[1]

Gallup. (2016). *Gallup student poll. Engaged today - Ready for tomorrow. Fall 2015 survey results*. Washington, DC: Author.

In terms of my own children, perhaps the difference is that what they're learning in school feels irrelevant to their lives, therefore causing them to tune out. It's possible that what or how they're learning isn't entirely engaging which also impacts intrinsic motivation. Educator-to-educator, I completely get it. There's no doubt that it requires a lot of work to craft relevant learning experiences that engage students at a high level. Reflecting on my earlier years of teaching, I'm guilty myself of periodically focusing more on the content I have to teach as opposed to creating experiences in which I know students learn best.

Taking the leap has required dedication, perseverance, and a phenomenal team to collaborate with to create top-notch learning that deeply engages students through cultivating their strengths and interests. There are creative ways we can bring these learning opportunities to fruition. In fact, many educators, myself included, work diligently to do so. It's time we collectively focus on creating relevant experiences rather than merely focusing on the dispersal of content.

What the Research Says

Cognitive psychology studies provide clinical evidence that stress, boredom, confusion, low motivation, and anxiety can individually, and more profoundly in combination, interfere with learning.[2] On the flipside, research points to the fact that superior learning takes place when classroom experiences are enjoyable and relevant to students' lives, interests, and personal experiences.[3] Based on the research, it's evident that creating learning experiences connected to students' lives and interests is critical not only to engage, but also enrich learning. Identifying our learners' strengths and interests allow us to craft relevant and meaningful learning opportunities.

Eager to take on the challenge of shifting Abby's mindset on learning to influence her trajectory, I vowed to go to great lengths to identify avenues in which I could cultivate learners' strengths and interests while also fostering agency. With relationships at the heart of all we do, I knew I had to begin there.

Learner Agency

Our role is not to simply transmit learning to our students, but foster the conditions that empower them to construct their learning. We want to support every learner; those who feel lost, stifled, and even those who are content in their learning journey. Learner agency is the act of developing the capacity to navigate one's own learning without relying on constant direction from others, mainly, teachers. Fostering agency requires educators to relinquish the control we are accustomed to having and transferring it to our learners to empower them as co-pilots of their learning. Education Reimagined shares, "Learner Agency thrives when learners know themselves, discover their own gifts, and develop themselves as self-confident lifelong learners."

Education Reimagined defines agency as:

> Learning that is characterized by learning agency recognizes learners as active participants in their own learning and engages them in the design of their experiences and the realization of their learning outcomes in ways appropriate for their developmental level. As such, learners have choice and voice in their educational experiences as they progress through competencies. Harnessing his or her own intrinsic motivation to learn, each learner strives to ultimately take full ownership of his or her own learning.[4]

Considering that we had already begun the shift toward creating a learner-centered environment, with an intentional emphasis on fostering learner agency, I knew we were on the right track toward empowering every learner to cultivate their strengths and interests in the classroom. It was critical that we intentionally demonstrated that each individual had worth and deeply mattered in our classroom.

Creating the Conditions to Foster Learner Agency

Often, learners are accustomed to compliance-based learning environments. Learner agency doesn't just happen with automaticity. Fostering agency requires us to nourish the environment of our classrooms, while continually tending to each stage of growth. Relationships breed trust, and in the absence of trust is fear. We simply cannot expect learners to step beyond their zone of comfort by exhibiting voice and choice if the environment doesn't support it. While there are endless options we can employ to foster relationships with learners, let's explore a handful that have proven to be successful because after all, relationships are the heartbeat to a healthy school; without them, we cannot make the desired progress.

Fostering Authentic Relationships with Learners

- ◆ Greet learners daily with a smile at the door and engage in authentic conversations based on their interests in and out of school. Even though this is mentioned in many books and blogs, it remains an underutilized approach that we can take advantage of daily.
- ◆ Facilitate morning meetings with a central focus each day. Early in the school year the teacher may select the focus, but as routines develop, empower learners to select the focus. As agency further develops, the topic could be open, encouraging learners to share anything of their choice with peers and then engaging in authentic conversations that bond learners relationally.
- ◆ Take time to work with small groups of learners or one-on-one. Not only does this cultivate relationships between individuals, but it also has a positive impact on learning.
- ◆ Write positive notes to the entire class, and then on occasion, surprise learners with individual notes too. Make note of their special qualities or highlight something that you saw them do well with. To clarify, what you write doesn't have to be regarding something they excelled at, it may be that you recognized how a particular student exhibited tenacity during a difficult moment or even overcame a struggle in a certain area.
- ◆ Maintain the dignity of your learners at all times. If possible, seek opportunities to laugh with them in a joking

manner to sideline any rifts. If you have to redirect their choices, do so in a subtle manner to keep their self-esteem intact, particularly in front of their peers.

◆ Be understanding of age appropriate behavior and avoid nitpicking students' choices to maintain complete control. The idea is to relinquish control and place a greater emphasis on fostering strengths.

The time and measures it requires to successfully foster authentic relationships vary from student-to-student and even class-to-class. As educators, we need to take the pulse of our learning environments to gauge if the culture is supporting learners to grow outside their comfort zone, then retool when necessary.

The art of cultivating relationships should be heavily embedded throughout each school day with intentionality. By interweaving learning experiences that inspire students to begin connecting the dots between their strengths and interests to further enhance culture, we foster deeper relationships in the meantime. In combination, these serve as the stepping stones to begin fostering learner agency and spark intrinsic motivation.

Every Child Has Unique Strengths

Despite the fact that the majority of educators would feel as though they'd won the lottery if handed a classroom of Logans, it's the Abby's of the world who intrigue me. Students like Abby fascinate me because they have chosen not to conform to "the way it is," and seem to be seeking the answer to, "how could it be?" Again, it's our choice to view learners through a positive, strengths-based lens, as opposed to a negative, non-conformist type lens.

Research in one study reveals that, "The least favorite students were the non-conformists who made up their own rules. Teachers tend to discriminate against highly creative students, labeling them as troublemakers."[5] Reflecting on the research, imagine how we may be negatively shaping learners or influencing the path they take in life by communicating in subtle ways that they're troublemakers. It's concerning that our labeling and communication could create a self-fulfilling prophecy for some. Perhaps as educators, we could reframe our thinking and view non-conformists, or highly creative learners as individuals who can create immense change if supported to navigate their journey through identifying and cultivating their unique strengths. Let's be cognizant to seek out the strengths of every individual intentionally.

Interestingly, in comparison, compliant learners who seek to appease their parents and teachers by passively following routines, are more favorable to have in class. Plain and simple, teaching learners who are compliant is significantly more manageable. However, compliance rarely shakes up the way we do things.[6] Cultivating an environment where every learner wholeheartedly believes they're of value unleashes untapped potential, particularly as they discover their strengths and interests and grasp that they have a place and purpose.

Fostering agency within a student-centered environment, rather than teacher centered, communicates that every learner profoundly matters. Unfortunately, traditionally speaking, schools have followed a more compliance-based model of teaching and learning where students spend their time focusing on what's directed by their teacher. Not only was Abby the product of a teacher-centered classroom, but she was the poster child of non-conformist learners, the creative thinker perceived as more of a problem to be solved, than a gift to be discovered.

According to Seth Godin, "Compliance is simple to measure, simple to test for and simple to teach. Punish non-compliance, reward obedience, and repeat."[7] But in today's world, with technology rapidly accelerating the way we do things, and the economy shifting, we desperately need to empower learners through fostering agency and connecting learners with their strengths and interests. There is no good reason why many educators are still dangling carrots in front of students to learn. What benefit does it create? If students are only learning to appease adults or earn rewards, we've got it wrong. Alfie Kohn reminds us, "The more that people are rewarded for doing something, the more likely they are to lose interest in whatever they had to do to get the reward."[8] Creating opportunities for learners to develop agency is a non-negotiable in today's classroom. Whether you have a set curriculum, mandated programs or learning standards to utilize, there are always a variety of ways to infuse learners' strengths and interests to create relevancy and increase learner agency.

Don Wettrick, educator and founder of Future Ready U reminds us that, "while the world is rapidly rewarding the risk takers, the disruptors, the outside of the box thinkers, our schools have been rewarding the compliant, the 'good kid' that repeats back the 'correct answer.' We've operated under the assumption that as long as our students get good grades, do what they're told, and get into college, there would be a job waiting for them. If you look at the data, this is no longer the truth. Our 'good students' are lacking the innovation, creativity, and entrepreneurial problem-solving skills that are the most demanded now by ALL companies. So we have thousands of recent graduates that did what they were told but have, a lack of marketable skills, no network, and few job prospects."[9]

Of course, there are elements of compliance that are necessary to maintain safety and the systems that are mandated to be in place. With that said, we want to ensure that we identify as many opportunities as possible to empower learners through cultivating strengths and interests.

Before going further, take a moment to reflect on this question: When educators look out at their learners, what's at the forefront of their minds?

While some of you see the vast and varying needs of learners, others may say they see unique individuals and the diversity that they bring to the table. However, due to the intense demands and expectations that are inevitable, the majority of educators who attend my conference sessions respond to this question by sharing that when they look at their learners they see all of the content, curriculum, and standards they're responsible for teaching. As an educator, I know this feeling all to well. The pressures are very real, and I'm not proposing that we neglect them.

However, there's no disputing that when students are motivated, learning becomes more productive, leading to richer results. We need to cultivate the disruptor and bust the compliance paradigm.

Encouraging Learners to Identify Personal Strengths

Activities that focus on supporting individuals to identify personal strengths communicates that it's okay to be you and that it's a great thing to be different, we want original thoughts and ideas to flourish. Learners also begin acknowledging commonalities amongst peers that they may not have realized without exploring what their strengths are and then sharing through conversation. All too often learners are influenced by pop culture and the media convincing them that they need to act, dress, or behave like those who influence the masses. Supporting learners to recognize their strengths assists in the development of confidence. Students begin to honor who they are as individuals, and this contributes to the transformation of the culture of learning.

This past year our team facilitated an activity titled, "The Best Part of Me," using Wendy Ewald's book, *The Best Part of Me*. While learners are encouraged in this activity to identify a positive physical trait of themselves and then craft a poem describing the best part of themselves, we wanted to form a deeper connection to their chosen trait based on why they feel it's the best part of who they are. Learners crafted beautiful poems detailing why their brain is the best part because it allows them to dream, question, create, and learn. Other learners voiced that their legs are their best part because they enable them to run speedily in baseball. In all transparency, though the final products were phenomenal, the beginning was sticky. Learners were unaccustomed to contemplating the best part of themselves. A few, including Abby, seemed thrown off by the activity and hesitant to share their opinions. Gradually, as their peers shared out, and through the incorporation of the mentor text to model, learners inched forward and honored different attributes of themselves. It was a beautiful moment as walls began to break down.

To scaffold the process of developing a positive self-image and increased confidence, we also leveraged lessons from Ignite Your S.H.I.N.E.®, founded and created by LaVonna Roth. Throughout the lessons, learners began to identify attributes pertaining to who they are as an individual, and connected with peers based on common traits. As we journeyed through the lessons, learners also recognized their special differences, and developed a greater understanding that we're all created differently. Learners embraced one another for that very purpose. It's enlightening when learners begin to view one another in a new light. For example, a child who's perceived as disruptive or who struggles with appropriate social interactions, may be recognized for their generosity, creativity, or ability to problem solve. We can shift how learners perceive themselves, including how they view others. Within learning, students identify the strengths of not only themselves, but their peers too, leading to the development of a cohesive, family-like, culture.

Creating opportunities for learners to be reflective of who they are, while helping them to grasp that what they have to contribute is appreciated, develops a sense of worth and value. We all can relate to the concept that feeling valued is a key ingredient to a healthy culture. People who feel valued are always more likely to do and give more as a result of being intrinsically motivated.

What are you currently doing to foster a learning environment that supports individuals to recognize their strengths and those of their peers, while demonstrating that everyone is of value?

Returning to Abby, while she had exhibited talent in many areas within school, she herself didn't seem to recognize her own strengths, let alone value them. Abby confided, "throughout school I've always felt like I'm not good enough. I don't think like the other kids, and I'm not interested in anything they talk about. Today I realized that I'm pretty special and have more to offer than I ever knew."

We are the difference makers who have greater influence than we may realize. Carving out the time to encourage learners to identify their strengths is simply invaluable.

Voice and Choice to Cultivate Strengths and Interests

Providing learners with plentiful opportunities to make decisions connected with their learning, catapults agency. When we encourage learners to take control, they begin tuning into their internal voice instead of seeking direction or frequent guidance from others. Our goal is to seize every opportunity to empower our compliant learners so they can recognize that their own ideas have value, while also fostering a culture where our nonconformist type learners flourish and feel a sense of belonging. It's simply critical that we support every learner to grasp that they're valued, have influence, and a sense of purpose.

Based on personal experiences and from working alongside fellow educators, it can be difficult for teachers to relinquish control, particularly if shifting toward student-centered learning is new. However, empowering learners to develop greater ownership fosters a more cohesive and collaborative classroom community where every learner recognizes themself as a contributor and leader of learning. Educators share that when shifting toward a student-centered classroom, it's best to start small with what you feel most comfortable and gain traction along the way by layering in new opportunities for learners.

In classrooms that foster agency, no longer is the teacher calling all of the shots, but learners are actively making decisions without seeking permission to move forward. There's not one educator I know who is excited about seeing passive learners simply sitting and awaiting the next direction. If we truly want our learners to be responsive to their own needs and capable of identifying what works best for them to learn at the deepest levels, we need to explore how we can support them.

Learners as Co-Designers of Their Learning Space

The creation or redesign of our learning environment is ideal when crafted with our learners' voices at the forefront of the conversation. When the learning environment is flexible, meaning that learners not only design the classroom, but restructure it as needed, we cultivate greater autonomy as students identify how they learn best and then employ what works. Supporting learners to be cognizant of how they learn best amplifies their ability to develop their strengths and interests as they become tuned into their needs and what works best for them as individuals.

A flexible environment elevates engagement as it encourages increased collaboration, communication, critical thinking, and creativity amongst learners. As learners gather in various groupings to discuss a topic, participate in a design challenge, engage in problem solving, or share ideas, we promote opportunities for them to learn from one another and build upon previous understandings. In our classroom, learners are empowered to reposition furniture as they see fit and even rearrange what's displayed around our classroom.

Every learning environment is unique, so it's important to identify how to include the voice of your unique learners. Connecting with educators over the years on social media, I've compiled a variety of ways in which we can empower learners to co-design their learning space.

Empowering Learners as Co-Designers

- ◆ Share with learners that their voice matters. Many educators, myself included, explicitly state to students that the classroom does not belong to *me*. It's not *mine*, it's *ours*. Our learning environment is our home, as we're a family.
- ◆ With learners, carve out time to explore all the various ways in which they may enjoy learning. Some examples may include: sitting, sprawling out on the floor, standing, or having the option to move when the need strikes.
- ◆ Open the floor for learners to share what type of seating they'd prefer to have in the classroom. You may need to provide options if the concept is new.
- ◆ If various seating options already exist, inquire if they have any additional suggestions.
- ◆ Resist placing names at seats as it communicates to learners that spot belongs to them and that they're expected to sit there.

◆ As for the walls of the classroom, invite learners to select what they want exhibited as long as it's not visually distracting. Perhaps they have specific work they're proud of and would like it displayed. Or, maybe they would like specific anchor charts hung in a certain location to be better utilized. In our classroom, learners took advantage of available wall space to display various selections of their artwork, too.

As learners develop the understanding that their voice is genuinely valued, and that the classroom *belongs* to all of them, relationships deepen. Sharing privileges with learners translates to feeling respected, and learners will therefore demonstrate mutual respect in return. Everything we do to communicate with learners connects back to relationships, which matter most.

Opportunities to Explore Strengths and Interests

Within our schools opportunities should exist that empower learners to explore their strengths and interests. If every minute of the day is scheduled for learners, we may be denying them of their right to construct their own knowledge through personal learning experiences. Sir Ken Robinson, author of *The Element* argues, "Whether or not you discover your talents and passions is partly a matter of opportunity. If you've never been sailing, or picked up an instrument, or tried to teach or to write fiction, how would you know if you had a talent for these things?"[10]

What opportunities currently exist for your learners to explore their strengths and interests?

How can we provide experiences that spark and then develop learners' interests?

In a recent study, Yale-NUS college psychologist Paul O'Keef shares, "Parents, teachers, and employers might get the most out of people if they suggest that interests are developed, not simply found. Telling people to find their passions could suggest that it's within you just waiting to be revealed." From

O'Keef's research it was identified that individuals who have a growth mindset have increased interest in areas outside of their pre-existing interest. O'Keef elaborates, "they [learners] might be seeing connections among new areas and the interest they already have." The research is clear that those with a growth mindset identify and develop interests more frequently than those with a fixed mindset. For example, according to the findings, individuals with a fixed mindset can have dangerous downsides, including a tendency to abandon interests when faced with any difficulties.[11]

While passions developed from strengths and interests can be a powerful driver of motivation, we can't ignore the research. For learners to identify strengths and passions, we must support the development of them, while also cultivating a growth mindset in learners.

A growth mindset is the ability to grasp that abilities are developed over time and that there are no limitations to growth and improvement. On the other hand, a fixed mindset is the belief that basic qualities such as their intelligence or talent, are fixed traits. Those with a fixed mindset avoid developing their talents and rationalize why they cannot do what they set out to do

Maker Education To Cultivate Strengths and Interests

In our journey to connect learners with their strengths and interests, and at the same time providing opportunities for learners to develop a growth mindset, we developed a schoolwide makerspace accessible to all staff and students. Makerspaces inspire learners to explore their curiosities, refine skills, and experiment with new designs or participate in challenges related to STEAM. Every makerspace, creation station, or fab lab is different from the next as what is offered should be based on the needs and interests of our learners.

Makerspaces may include:

◆ A wide variety of arts and crafts materials
◆ LEGO, Tinker Toys, and other similar resources

- Tools to both construct and deconstruct
- Materials such as old keyboards or printers to take apart and explore
- Robotics for all age groups
- Coding gadgetry
- Sewing equipment
- Video creation and editing tools
- Resources to create and publish books or comics
- Mini-greenhouse activities for growing plants or flowers
- Musical creation station
- Sensory activities
- Anything your learners can imagine that connect to identified interests or that will spark curiosity

Opportunities to Explore and Create

For learners to identify and further explore their strengths and interests, it's imperative that we provide opportunities to do so. Laura Fleming, educator and author of *The Kickstart Guide to Making Great Makerspaces* shared with me that their "students are free to visit their makerspace when they can, and when they want to, and no one tells them what to do when they get there." Students in their school have complete autonomy to explore and cultivate their interests. Fleming also shared that their school moved to a rotating block schedule which has opened even more opportunities for learners to participate in maker education.

In our classroom, learners explore and develop their strengths and interests daily. Abby gets all the credit for the launch of what we call, maker mornings. Even though our school has a fantastic makerspace, going once or twice per week wasn't enough. Considering that students were empowered to co-design our learning space, Abby spoke up one day and said, "why can't our classroom be a makerspace?" Scanning the room, I noticed the eyes of every learner light up! As their eyes met one another, I could tell they were considering all of the possibilities. Their energy and initiative to learn was incredibly contagious.

Later that same day, a team decided to begin the process of designing our classroom makerspace. Collaboratively we decided to utilize counter space and a section of cabinets in our classroom to store materials, and dedicate the first 25 minutes of each day to exploring and developing strengths and interests. Maker mornings kicked off with basic and accessible materials, along with donations from families and myself. If you're seeking greater funding, look into DonorsChoose.org for support.

Shifts require us to reimagine what's possible to create new and improved opportunities. In our case, it was a simple case of empowering the voices of learners and not just listening, but honoring their ideas. Maker education supports learners to identify their strengths and interests, and then build on them, "but fostered" is critical thinking, collaboration, communication, and creativity as learners leverage various opportunities to explore and learn.

Lasting Impression; Lifetime of Impact

Throughout our year, I watched Abby blossom. From cynical and aloof to charismatic and personable, Abby flourished as she recognized and developed her unique strengths and interests. Learners embraced one another for their individuality and walls that often separate learners on the foundation of labels or cliques, crumbled. Albert Einstein famously said:

> The most valuable thing a teacher can impart to children is not knowledge and understanding per se but a longing for knowledge and understanding, and an appreciation for intellectual values, whether they be artistic, scientific, or moral. It is the supreme art of the teacher to awaken joy in creative expression and knowledge. Most teachers waste their time by asking questions that are intended to discover what a pupil does not know, whereas the true art of questioning is to discover what the pupil does know or is capable of knowing.

Our role goes far beyond preparing learners to simply be successful in the next grade level, move on to college or become employed. While we can acknowledge that each is important, ultimately it doesn't transfer to creating a lasting impact on learners. Join me as we ditch the compliance-based paradigm of learning by cultivating the strengths and interests of learners and fostering agency. Together we can take the leap and transform learning experiences to inspire students to develop the drive to learn. Let's open the gateway to unlimited possibilities where every individual is encouraged to flourish. *We* are the difference makers, and it's essential we take the leap.

Notes

1. Gallup Report, www.longviewoneducation.org.
2, 3. www.psychologytoday.com/files/attachments/4141/ the-neuroscience-joyful-education-judy-willis-md.pdf.
4. https://education-reimagined.org/wp-content/uploads/ 2018/06/A-transformational-vision-for-education-in-the-U.S.- Logo-Updated.pdf.
5. Grant, A., & Sandberg, S. (2017). *Originals: How non-conformists move the world.* New York: Penguin Publishing Group, p.10.
6. Grant, A., & Sandberg, S. (2017). *Originals: How non-conformists move the world.* New York: Penguin Publishing Group, p.9.
7. Seth Godin (2012, October 16). STOP STEALING DREAMS: Seth Godin at TEDxYouth@BFS. Retrieved from www. youtube.com/watch?v=sXpbONjV1Jc.
8. Kohn, A. (2006). *Unconditional parenting: Moving from rewards and punishments to love and reason.* New York: Atria, p.33.
9. www.futurereadyu.com/.
10. www.forbes.com/sites/danschawbel/2013/06/05/sir-ken-robinson-how-to-discover-your-true-talents/#75a17a762553.
11. https://qz.com/1314088/find-your-passion-is-bad-advice-say-yale-and-stanford-psychologists/?utm_source=Facebook& utm_medium=organic&utm_campaign=k-12.

Resources

www.scholastic.com/teachers/lesson-plans/teaching-content/best-
    part-me/.
www.igniteyourshine.com.

5

ParentCamp

Filling the Relationship Gap Between Schools and Families

Laura Gilchrist

In 2017 I served on an education panel for TechWeekKC. Six of us talked for over two hours with the audience of fifty people. The audience members, mostly in technology careers, asked many questions. They were into this community conversation and so were we. In fact, once we hit the Q and A, there wasn't a time a hand wasn't up. One of the themes I spoke about during the panel was how to improve family school community engagement in schools. One of the members in the audience, who happened to be a parent, raised his hand and shared a frustration that many of us have had but perhaps have never considered, thanks to 'the way things have always been done' in parent engagement. He said the following:

> If I have an idea or proposal I think would be good for the kids in my neighborhood school, what do I do, go to the Principal's Office?

There was a pause. You know that pause when people in a crowd come to a realization at the same time. Heads were nodding.

It was almost as if they were thinking, "Yea, really, where do you go to talk about education in our school?"

Are you happy with your school's family-school engagement? Does it feel right? Can't put your finger on it? You're not alone.

What do you believe is the missing piece in family school or parent engagement that, if we got it right, would allow us to flip a school from fortress school to partnership school – a community hub that shines from the inside out?

It's not an easy process but I'll tell you something. It's not that difficult either. The hardest part is always the beginning.

Why are schools and parents isolated and almost fearful of each other; not freely talking, planning, and creating? Fear is not something you build on. Fear breeds isolation. Fear breeds fear. Fear breeds a closed mindset.

Let's stop managing parents and families and start leading with them!

To do that, we must interact and converse with them freely about a wide variety of things. We will build trust and relationships. Those trusting relationships will open the doors to new ways of being a learning community with, completely new outcomes.

In my experience, most education planning is done through curriculum teams and it's done with teachers and administrators in a structured way that usually doesn't involve the living breathing world beyond the walls of the school. The community and city are the context, the setting of the kids' lives. Parents, students, families, and community members are not involved with teachers and administrators in dynamic planning of new and relevant experiences. It's on teachers' shoulders to plan the learning that is ideally city based and as varied as possible. And let me tell you, teachers can't do it alone and for the kids' sake they shouldn't have to. They can't. Education is an all-of-us-endeavor!

Every school has a powerful and rich resource right under its nose, right in its backyard – and that resource is its own family network. This family network has skill and talent, kindness and caring, and access to businesses and opportunities, all of which can provide rich immersive experiences providing our kids with new perspectives and ideas to inform their futures. Perspectives and experiences are exactly what build empathy and fuel the inner, growing learner.

Parents and families are our kids' first and original **teachers and champions**! We want our kids to feel a sense of belonging and connection to their entire community of adults, inside the school and out.

It's time for schools, yes schools, to go all in and champion family-school engagement. But how? I will share a structure that is free and easy to implement that will help your school take the first step in family school-engagement and capacity building. We have a lot of ground to cover to move from fortress schools to partnership schools, two types of schools described in the book, *Beyond the Bake Sale* (Henderson & Mapp, 2007).

Imagine This at YOUR School

Teachers, family members of all ages, and community members meet once per month either after school in the evening or on a Saturday for 1.5 hours or so to talk about ideas families indicate they wanted to talk, learn, and plan about. Everyone has choice, voice, and the opportunity for multitudes of two-way conversations. Each monthly ParentCamp event is not spent listening to presenters. It is spent talking, laughing, planning, learning, and walking out the doors feeling alive and excited. The entire night was spent growing together for kids!

In one month you can put one on at your school. I'll show you how in this chapter. ParentCamp will build the capacity in your school that will take it to the next level!

ParentCamps create the one vital thing that's missing between schools and families, and that is relationships.

Teach to the Heart – And What's INSIDE of it!

If you could peek into the eyes of a child in your classroom and see what's inside their heart, what would you see?

You would see families. You'd see moms and dads, step-moms and step-dads, grandmas and grandpas, uncles and aunts, sisters and brothers, cousins and pets.

You'd see teachers and coaches, friends and neighbors, counselors and clergy. You'd see people they've bonded with through repeated connections and two-way interactions – something we call RELATIONSHIPS. The quality of the bonding/relationships depends on the quantity and quality of the immersion experiences.

The heart and soul of every child is his or her family and friends from school and community.

- ◆ If we value our students, we value what's in their hearts.
- ◆ If we value what's in their hearts, we embrace and partner with their families and friends! In doing so, we elevate our students' individual and collective sense of belonging, mattering, learning, and voice.

But wait, it gets better!

It follows that whatever we do for family and friends to build capacity, empowerment, and belonging – we **ALSO do for kids.** Kids follow what they see in their families and friends.

- ◆ **When we develop family and friends, we develop kids.** For instance, if parents learn a new parenting skill with us at a ParentCamp or other learning event, the new practice implemented at home by the parent positively impacts the child(ren). BONUS!! YES!!
- ◆ **When we engage with family and friends, we engage with kids.** When we ask for their needs and wishes, when we identify parents as allies, parents feel included and happy. This happiness is passed on to kids at home.
- ◆ **When we invite family and friends to the education innovation table, we invite students.** When parents help guide a new program or idea, their input is most

closely connected to the kids. The outcome will likely be better because of it. Plus parents and students talk (and students will likely end up at this table as your school gets going).

◆ **When we ignore family and friends, we ignore kids. Truly.** When we ignore important people in our kids' hearts and they feel unvalued, those important people speak negatively, from hurt or fear, and carry negative body language about school. Kids follow what they see adults doing and expressing. This negative view becomes the kids' view.

◆ What does it feel like to you if you replace "family and friends" – with teachers?!

Does it Matter What We Call It?

Since the words we use determine our thoughts, emotions and mindsets, let's pause a moment and inventory the commonly used phrases enabling you to make an informed decision on what you prefer to call it.

Which phrases will lead us to inclusive and interconnected engagement practices that uplift kids, parents/families and community. Which phrases lead us the wrong way?

In an ideal world the people in a child's heart – parents, families, teachers, friends and community members – would be connected to each other in relationships. These people would communicate and partner in a dynamic and positive way all year long. They would together focus on learning, creating, nurturing and nudging the child into his/her future! They would create access to a flow of opportunities and happiness and belonging, all of which nurture self-identity and self-love.

Let's start with "Parent Communication." This is a term I hear a lot. "We need to increase our communication to parents." This term causes a little alarm bell to go off in my mind because 1) it sounds like a chore, 2) it sounds 1-way and 3) my mind goes to traditional status quo practices like phone calls and emails, perhaps meetings. It doesn't go to happy people talking, meeting, and asking to meet more!!

"Parent engagement" and "Parent involvement" seem to call up a sense of interaction with parents and school where Communication does not.

Let's zoom out. Bigger picture. Bigger word count.

"Family-School Engagement" shows the connection between not only parents but also families WITH school. I use this frequently.

"Family School Community Engagement" is the most comprehensive and in my eyes the best to use because it elicits in our minds the goal – impacting and engaging the entire context of a child's world and the entire ecosystem of support and resources around them. As an educator, my mind starts seeing the big picture, pushing my purview beyond the school walls. The amount of time it takes to type this phrase keeps me from using it consistently.

Karen Mapp, Harvard Graduate School of Education, refers to it as Family-School Engagement. I choose to use the phrases interchangeably throughout this chapter of EdWriteNow and in my everyday talk.

Ineffective Family School Partnerships

I believe it would be fair to say that many schools in the United States have **ineffective family school partnerships.** This is what Karen Mapp's Dual Frameworks for Effective Family-School Engagement states.

I appreciate the word "ineffective" because of its objectivity. When something is ineffective, we can do things to move along the continuum toward effective. When something is bad, the charge of judgment clouds our thinking and planning.

Ineffective family school partnerships are not the schools' fault. They're not a teacher's fault or a principal's fault either. Nor are they the parents' fault. Both schools and parents will often blame the other for apathy or lack of communication. When both sides are unhappy and the blame game is happening, we know it's time to reassess and redesign. While they're no one's fault, it is the school's responsibility to strategically change it.

What is the basis of the dysfunction, the apathy, the lack of engagement and excitement between parents, family, and educators?

>It comes down to relationships. Relationships Matter, People!

To build relationships you must spend time together talking, laughing. You must be able to talk about things you are interested in. You must have open time to interact.

But can we truly move from apathy to joyful partnerships? How do you build relationships, anyway? How do we start?

My Experiences with Family-School Engagement

During Parent-Teacher conferences, which happened once a year, I would meet with the parents of approximately 25 of my 100 students. The students would lead the conferences. The conversations and interactions between the three of us – teacher, parent(s), student – were usually positive and empowering, reflective and goal oriented. Two-way, back and forth conversation occurred in the short 15–20 minute window we had. The parent and student often walked out with head held higher thanks to a **shared family-school bond around learning and the learner**!

Shocking. If I met with 25 of the 100 students' parents in two-way conversation around learning, that means I **did not meet with** the other 75 students' parents in that way. There were likely parents on every team that I would not EVER have a face to face conversation with or even SEE in person. That doesn't feel right, does it? It feels disrespectful of parents but also of the students. In a perfect world, it would be ideal to talk and join with parents and families frequently around learning and students.

It was always done that way: I could never shake the idea that the main opportunity parents had during the year for face-to-face, two-way conversations with teachers was parent-teacher conference night. It is likely that during those 20 years as a science and social studies teacher, my mind was comfortable with the pattern of conferences and events, and some of the daily one-way communication my team sent out to parents via email. The pattern was the same when I was growing up. I'll bet you it was the same when my parents were in school and yours.

There's a wealth of resources, ideas, skills in our parents, right? Would parents share and volunteer if we asked them? If we started learning or design conversations with them, would they be interested in being "at the education table"? New questions surfacing. A new way of thinking and partnering is opening up, even though it's been right under our noses the entire time.

Parent engagement was a separate thing. It has been addressed as such in all my years in education.

The onus of parent engagement was placed on teachers rather than school or district driving it through overall strategy. It was a lot of one-way communication – that was parent engagement.

As a teacher I was expected to call home x number of times per quarter. The way it is phrased, it felt like an assignment to me rather than a joyful partnership opportunity. Do phone calls have to be solely about grades or behavior? There's so little time and phone calls are not face-to-face. Why not schedule more face-to-face events to build real relationships and partnerships?

"Be sure to call home x number of times per quarter."

Phone calls are two way conversation. However, the agenda is set by the teacher. The teacher is calling for a reason. The parents are responding. It's not typically an open dialogue around parents questions, ideas, thoughts. Wouldn't that be fun to do, though?

Communication Gap/Relationship Gap

The way kids and adults learn best is through inductive, open-ended exploration first, to gain perspectives and soak your senses in the new experience. Next follows deductive thinking, analysis and further extension. This is exciting learning. Our schools are filled with mostly deductive, decontextualized learning experiences.

This chart has been my way of processing for my lessons and I find that it works for adult and community learning as well.

Immersive Experiential Experiences	⇨	Bonding/ Relationships	⇨	Love & Deep Learning	⇨	Leading from the Love & Learning
This is ParentCamp		This is ParentCamp		ParentCamp relationships lead to this		ParentCamp relationships lead to this

The way it is in many schools: Family-School Engagement is difficult and feels stressful to both educators and parents. Family-School Engagement is an add-on, seen as separate from the school's identity; parents are viewed as something to manage. Schools and parents are separate from each other, interacting when they have to from their silo, their side of the gap. From the educator perspective, we know the fear of being on the receiving side of an angry parent who is lost in emotion. From the parent perspective, we know the feeling of sting of lack of information or feeling of uncaring treatment of a child. Both sides feel unvalued by the other.

Problems:

◆ Lack of connecting opportunities, conversations, and relationships between educators and families.
◆ Schools do not strategically communicate and partner with parents beyond the status quo of parent/teacher conferences, events, and phone calls. The communication is largely managerial and about grades, behavior, dates for events, field trips.

♦ Schools do not ask parents for input, their talents, their hopes, their ideas, their needs/concerns.

♦ Schools are not welcoming places to parents; sign-in process and offices that are cold and unwelcoming; come only if you call and have a reason.

♦ One-way communication is most common from the school, from teachers. Parents and families are passive participants in Family-School Engagement. It is being done to them.

♦ Increasing the number of one-way communications from school to family does not make a thriving family-school engagement.

♦ Parent engagement strategy should not be teacher phone calls.

Result:

♦ Schools do not communicate with parents well, or include them; schools do not invest in engaging parents.

♦ Parents and families come to the opportunities and events the schools offer.

♦ Are we okay with what's being offered? Is this really all there is?

During my 20 years as a middle school science and social studies teacher, I knew in my heart there had to be more to "parent engagement" than Parent-Teacher Conference night, Back-to-School Night, student performance events like sports, and parent information nights. Three of the four examples above consisted of one-way communication from either teachers or students TO parents. This type of communication places parents in the passenger seat, as passive consumers rather than active contributors. Choice and voice are not options for parents. Who benefits from passive parents or parents who are not asked or engaged? Who is diminished in this communication format?

What causes schools to fear communicating and partnering with parents in different ways and around parents' and families' interests? There's no different model. We haven't SEEN anything different. It's what we grew up with.

We need to change. Lack of rich two-way conversational communication results in feelings of disconnection, isolation, diminishment, and oppression.

The good news: Families and schools can become JOYFUL ALLIES, working together for our kids – because we want to and we can! We can create a new and beautiful reality together around our kids. Our community can experience exponential growth and feelings of belonging, value, and worth.

Our job as educators: Uncover the implicit status quo mindset and beliefs keeping us locked into management of, rather than engagement with, parents. The silo effect. Ask the parents what they want and need. Do something to make it reality!

Ask the parents & community the following questions. Better yet—ask the PARENTS & COMMUNITY!! They have the answers!:

- What is the elephant in the room with parents and families?
- What is it parents and families really want to learn, discuss, plan? What is it they fear?
- What do parents and families need from schools and teachers?
- Are we providing ample time/place for face-to-face conversations with all parents?
- **What if we asked parents what they wanted to learn, talk about or do . . . and then made it happen? (Doesn't seem like rocket science – more like design thinking.)**
- What makes parents feel we don't value them?
- Is there a better way?
- What is it we are scared of or unsure of regarding parents and co-creating with them?
- What are examples of schools with high functioning parent engagement?
- How can we get started and not feel overwhelmed?

A Framework for what EFFECTIVE Family-School Engagement Looks Like?

Parent participation is the leading predictor that supports students' academic success, regardless of race, socioeconomic status, ethnicity, or cultural background.

Karen Mapp, Faculty Chair (Karen L. Mapp, Ed.D., is a senior lecturer on education at the Harvard Graduate School of Education (HGSE) and the faculty director of the Education Policy and Management Master's Program).

Parent and family agency.
Parent and family leadership.
Schools shining from the inside out.

Back in 2014, Joe Mazza launched a Voxer book study group. We read *Beyond the Bake Sale,* by Anne T. Henderson, Karen L. Mapp, Vivian R. Johnson, Don Davies. ParentCamp was born out of that book study and out of Joe Mazza's own ParentCamp at the elementary school at which he was principal. The core beliefs of parents, which I read daily are the following:

- ◆ **Core Belief #1:** All parents have dreams for their children and want the best for them.
- ◆ **Core Belief #2:** All parents have the capacity to support their children's learning.
- ◆ **Core Belief #3:** Parents and school staff should be equal partners.
- ◆ **Core Belief #4:** The responsibility for building partnerships between school and home rests primarily with school staff, especially school leaders.

When you read these core beliefs, do you feel yourself saying YES?!

Four types of Schools according to *Beyond the Bake Sale*: Fortress School, Come if We Call School, Open Door School, and

Partnership School. You want to become a Partnership School. It is possible. It's a matter of intentional planning and action . . . and taking the first steps.

We can move from a Fortress School or Come if We Call School to a Partnership School. The thing we must face is – each other. In immersive contextual and interest-driven conversations and learning opportunities to better ourselves so we can better our kids and ultimately make a thriving community that will self-sustain and scale!

For more, read about **The Dual Capacity-Building Framework** by Dr. Karen Mapp, Harvard Graduate School of Education. It describes the conditions needed to move from ineffective to effective family student engagement geared around student achievement and school improvement. It is about building conditions and capacity in the system, for growth. www2. ed.gov/documents/family-community/partnership-frame works.pdf).

What is ParentCamp?

I'm going to share one simple but effective way to get started building capacity so school districts can move from ineffective to effective family-school engagement. It's called ParentCamp (www.parentcamp.org). It's designed after the Edcamp Model (www.edcampfoundation.org). ParentCamp is an unconference built around what the parents want to talk about or learn about. The actual attendees are parents, teachers, administrators, and community. Children, too!

If I had a magic wand, **your school** and every other school would do at least one ParentCamp in the next year, and ideally more!

A ParentCamp costs nothing. It is a simple structure for building relationships and hearing/valuing perspectives and skillsets or other assets each person has. The relationships open the doors to new realities. You, yes you, can host a ParentCamp at your school or district one month from today with almost no expense. Reflections and testimonials from parents, teachers, and administrators who have experienced and/or setup a parent-camp will give you a vision of what you can FEEL and gain from every ParentCamp.

What if we invited and welcomed families to the education planning table at each school – for conversations, and dinners, for planning together amazing learning for our kids that is embedded in community?! What if schools asked parents monthly what they wanted to learn, discuss, create, and do and then invited them to conversations where they had choice and voice? We could be Joyful Allies, working together to give our kids amazing opportunities that couldn't be possible through just the teachers or just the families.

Is there a place for divergent thinking, for community based learning projects that could be developed, or for instance, connecting kids with entrepreneurs in your city to solve a problem or start a business?

We need the following that doesn't exist widely – at all. Parents need a place, time, and intentional seeking seat at the education planning table at local schools that involves regular curating of resources from the community or intentional. It's no one's fault. Family-school or parent engagement is possibly one of the last movers in innovation. Schools are afraid of parent engagement, possibly afraid of conflict. It is an opportunity for parents to talk and ideate. Parents, teachers, and community members sitting in a circle talking about things parents wanted to talk about.

What do you Talk About at a ParentCamp?

◆ You talk about things the parents want to talk about. Period. Always.

ParentCamp builds real relationships and drops the walls between family and school. People leave happy!
<u>**Yes you can launch a ParentCamp one month from today!**</u>
Thinking of ParentCamp as a difficult, time consuming or overwhelming event is simply not necessary! Drop the old script. It is actually quite simple, with most of the work coming behind the scenes – with the survey and finding facilitators. The actual

day of ParentCamp is about talking and celebration and wondering when you'll do another one! With some organizing tips and a school/parentcamp support team, you will seize the day! You cannot "mess it up." ParentCamp board is here for you via Voxer, Email, Google Hangout, Direct Message, etc!

About the planning lift: The bulk of the work of parentcamp is before the ParentCamp! The ParentCamp itself is easy and incredible. Show up and go!!

Launch a ParentCamp in One Month: Just Do It!

What makes ParentCamp different from traditional parent events?:

- ♦ **Law of Two Feet**
    - ♦ Participants may go where they choose, when they choose. It is a time to be "selfish" as a learner, as a parent-leader. Parents LOVE this. They have choice.
    - ♦ "It's your day to be selfish as a parent leader and parent learner. Go where you grow. You will not offend a presenter when you get up. Talking in the hall during a session is part of go where you grow. It's okay. We encourage networking anywhere at anytime."
- ♦ **Law of 2-Way Conversation:** Facilitators (you choose them ahead of time) are encouraged to bring three key questions to the 25 minute sessions, then nurture and guide the conversation and connecting! Facilitators expect that people will get up during a session and go anywhere else because they know the day is about the learners.
- ♦ **Based on parent/community needs survey each time**: Think in terms of tracks: learning, innovation, careers, whole child. You'll create a list of topic choices for parents to choose, perhaps in a learning and an innovation track. Parents choose the top three in each. Then, you MUST add an open ended question where parents can add a topic.
- ♦ **When you DEVELOP the parent, you develop the child.**

Fears Educators have about ParentCamp: Top Two Questions

- **What if parents yell, get angry?** Basically, they don't and you handle it like you would during the day.
- **What if no one shows up?** They will. Be sure to email and make it sound amazing – as it will be. Even 20 showing up is a win. This is not about numbers, it's about the experience together.
- There is nothing to fear except fear itself. You have everything to gain.

Before beginning you need: Buy-in, green light from Superintendent or Principal.

Plan team: Small team of teachers & principals to do the following:

Who to invite

- Parents, teachers, administrators, superintendents, community (and even kids!).
- If you only invite parents, you have a silo of just parents. The point is family-school engagement. You need everyone.

Where

- Use your school, or other location of your choice.
- Stockton USD 271 in Kansas used the four corners of the gym. Round tables in each corner.
- Parentcamp Kentucky used auditorium and classrooms.

How many rooms and what session titles

- You look at the total number signed up. Good rule of thumb is to divide by 10 to determine number of topics to offer by in each 25 minute session.

When

◆ 2 hours is all you need! Two to four 25-minute sessions!

TABLE 5.1 Schedule example #1 THREE 25-minute sessions

9–9:15	Mingle and breakfast/coffee
9:15–9:30	Welcome & Intro
9:35–10:05	Session 1
10:10–10:40	Session 2
10:45–11:15	Session 3
11:15–11:30	Reflect, Door prizes, Celebrations, Next steps!

TABLE 5.2 Schedule example #2 THREE 25-minute sessions

6–6:15	Welcome & Intro
6:20–6:45	Session 1
6:50–7:15	Session 2
7:20–7:45	Session 3
7:45–8:00	Reflect, Door prizes, Celebrations, Next steps!

TABLE 5.3 Schedule example #3 TWO 25-minutes sessions

5:30–5:45	Mingle and dinner—pizza, subs, etc.
5:45–6:20	Welcome & Intro + Speaker or Celebration or Student Presentation
6:30–6:55	Session 1
7:00–7:25	Session 2
7:25–7:30	Reflect, Door prizes, Celebrations, Next steps!

What do you talk about

◆ You talk about things the parents want to talk about. Period. Always. You find out by sending an email with both a survey and registration before each parentcamp. There is an art to the survey. I like this practice of reaching out to parents for what they want and need to learn.

Low tech – Don't *encourage* people to be on phones, computers: less worry. It's okay if they are are but no pressure. Encourage students or a few key educators to document via photos/videos and possibly interviews of parents before and after.

Day of Parentcamp – Post finalized session board (paper chart or on the wall via projector) with session names – and put up at school for parents/teachers to look at! Easy. Feel free to share it via tech, but do have visuals.

Gifts at the end that are a hit – Inspirational, leadership, parenting BOOKS. Put a name tag in a hat/basket at the end. . . . drawings for items above. ParentCamp is free with no vendors in booths (no pressure).

The Big 3: ParentCamp Planning!

1. <u>Parent Survey+Registration</u>
    a) Keep it simple: Use a Google or Microsoft form that contains both survey AND registration!
    b) Make sure to keep it open ended so you don't restrict too much. Themes are fine, but analyze with several sets of eyes the phrasing and setup of the survey. (We will help!)
        i) **Education** (careers of the future, parenting, STEM)
        ii) **Innovation** (redesign, social emotional learning, parent involvement in education design, how parents can be involved in school beyond room parent)
        iii) **Whole-Child** (Social-Emotional, Well-being, soft skills, mental health)
    c) Ideas for session tracks (identifying tracks is not necessary, can restrict)
    d) Build the session topics from their feedback
    e) **Determine number of sessions per time slot**. This depends on the number of parents and thus is dependent on your registration (and marketing) (average of 10/room is good rule of thumb for parentcamp, but you can do 15 if needed)

f) High interest topics. . . . do not be afraid to put them in two time slots!

2. **All Star Facilitators** from your city/community/schools

a) Phone calls rule – the process of finding ParentCamp facilitators will help you deepen ties to community!
b) Send follow up email with details of ParentCamp and when to arrive; bring three questions, etc.
c) Thank you – note, gift, media thank you
d) FACILITATOR GUILDELINES – ask questions; keep conversations going!

3. **SHARE the Heck out of it . . .**

Share your genuine excitement for your ParentCamp through Email, Social Media, Fliers, Next Door app, Videos – start to end!

a) Use your PTA, connected parents, and orgs to put it in their email lists
b) Share on Facebook and NextDoor app (if used in your area)
c) KEY – send out ParentCamp invite along with survey-registration link **repeatedly** via multiple district sources!
d) Fliers up in local businesses, orgs
e) PHONE CALLS – don't be afraid to call and invite people!
f) Idea: Create *Facebook Group* connected to the parent-camp Facebook page – for parents, attendees to talk, bounce ideas! We'll help you create and manage it.

After ParentCamp

You'll want to get feedback from all attendees to inform your next steps. Give a post-ParentCamp survey right at the end of ParentCamp and/or send it in email. Hold a strategic meeting within the next two weeks to share experiences, mine the parent and community survey feedback, and celebrate. Of course, your ultimate goal is to determine if and when your next ParentCamp will be held.

Take the most important step—First Step:

Give It a Try!

I know all schools genuinely want to have dynamic family-schoolcommunity engagement. A place to BEGIN, that's simply pedagogy, something you already know and do—is ParentCamp.

Go to www.parentcamp.org to sign up, get the free toolkit. We've found schools request virtual and/or on-site coaching for their first ParentCamp. It is available if you would like it, but you can do it yourself! To see ParentCamps in progress check out the #parentcamp hashtag and #edwritenow hashtags!

I believe in ParentCamp so much that I'm committed to spreading this unconference model for family-schoolcommunity engagement worldwide. I have seen the hope and happiness it brings in one two-hour session.

And now a memo from my longtime teacher heart! Helping schools start ParentCamps is my way to still be involved with kids—with my former kids. I hope to transform the familyschool-community engagement experience for my 2000 KIDS and their children. Of course, it goes without saying my own grandkids are another reason for doing this.

Reference

Henderson, Johnson, Mapp, & Davies (2007). *Beyond the Bake Sale: The Essential Guide to Family-School Partnerships.* New York: The New Press.

6

Connecting with Others Through Productive Conflict

Sanée Bell

Conflict. Just hearing the word or seeing it in print has the tendency to conjure negative emotions, thoughts, or memories. The word by sheer meaning is negative, and if left to stand alone without any additional qualifiers, is a word that offers little hope, peace, positivity, or closure. Conflict denotes that there will be winners and losers, and those who are able to voice their opinions or views the loudest will claim stake to victory. Conflict forces one to choose sides, hold on to narrow perspectives, and engage in unproductive dialogue that doesn't lead to better solutions.

Conflict does have its place in the world. There are just some fundamental truths and moral practices on which we must stand firm; but as educators, how can we reframe conflict into an activity that will result in the best possible outcomes and solutions for the students we serve? Is it possible to engage in productive conflict, which for this chapter means the sharing and acceptance of divergent ideas, perspectives, and experiences, to get the best solutions to the challenges and problems that plague our education system?

Engaging in productive conflict is not only necessary but it is critical to reimagining an educational system that is committed to fostering and developing high-performing teams that know how to engage productively with those who have differing perspectives and experiences. Without productive conflict, one is not able to grow or be challenged cognitively or philosophically. Refinement only happens through the convergence of new ideas and experiences. In fact, without productive conflict the best ideas will never be presented which will result in more of the same. Embracing the struggle and dissonance that will occur, while also practicing the art of vulnerability, is the only way that productive conflict will lead to positive outcomes.

Conflict as a Catalyst for Change

In my career as an educator, I have worked on a number of teams. Some of my fondest memories include working on a team that I felt genuinely connected to socially and professionally. We enjoyed each other's company, which made the work environment positive and upbeat. One could say that the team chemistry was a once in a lifetime experience or that it was formed out of "luck." When I think back on that team, I cannot articulate what we did to create such synergy and cohesiveness, but what I do know is that whatever it was did not happen through intentional planning. Creating an environment where productive conflict can thrive must be intentionally developed and consistently nurtured.

When I was a kid, we used to sing this song at church about the wise man who built his house on a rock. I am sure this took a great deal of time and probably was grueling work, but the wise man was well prepared when the rain came tumbling down. His counterpart, the foolish man, built his house on the sand. This building process probably was quicker to design and execute, but when the rain came down his design was not stable enough to provide adequate shelter from the storm. This same parable can be referenced when we think about the foundations we develop when working with others. Conflict is a critical step in the change process, but without establishing a solid foundation on which each team member feels valued, respected, trusted, and heard, productive conflict cannot be achieved.

Conflict as a Gateway to Authentic Relationships

Forming a team is the first step in establishing an environment for productive conflict. Engaging in productive conflict can be somewhat easier and happen more naturally when there are similar personalities, interests, and members have self selected themselves to be a part of the team; however, in most educational settings, team members are put together and are expected to work cohesively to accomplish a goal that is usually identified and measured outside of the members of the team. Far too often when teams are thrust together, the building of relationships does not go deeper than having surface level knowledge about the individuals with whom you may be working. Time does not permit teams to delve into the relationship work that is pivotal to building high-performing teams. Team dynamics change each time a new member is added to the team and far too often the time is not spent resetting the team. The new member of the team is forced to join the journey the team is currently on without any regard for their individual needs, values, and what they are bringing to the table.

It has been my personal experience that when leaders are not intentional about taking the time to build relationships and identify the strengths and styles each member brings to the table, frustration, disappointment and lack of progress toward goals will be inevitable. As a leader, my lack of focus on this issue caused a great deal of conflict and frustration for a team I was leading. It was my responsibility to set the tone and cultivate the culture of the team, and because of needing to get the work done, I did not remain consistent in my responsibility of building relationships with each individual and the team collectively. I had expectations that I assumed were clear to everyone, and I used my work ethic and way of processing as the only context to view situations and solutions. I was not patient with the process, which resulted in the development of unintentional barriers to our success. Building relationships on a deeper level takes effort, intentionality and a clearly defined path.

Relationships as the Cornerstone of Productive Conflict

The crux of any high-performing team is the team's commitment to building relationships. I would venture to say that teams who are truly committed to the work and each other is what propels them from being a good team to a great team. Good is the enemy of great because being good is safer than doing the hard work of what it takes to be great.

In order to move beyond the superficial relationships that are typically formed in school settings, there are some explicit activities that must occur before the core work begins. It is also critical to understand that although building relationships is time consuming, it is absolutely necessary. In fact, not taking the time to build relationships is sure to be a detriment to the team.

In the beginning stages, it is important for each member of the team to identify his or her strengths. Understanding and respecting personal strengths adds value to the team and gives each member the opportunity to highlight what they bring to the table as a team member. I recommend using a strengths-based assessment that produces a profile of strengths for each individual. This not only gives each individual the opportunity to become more self-aware of their personal strengths, but sharing this profile can give team members an in-depth insight into the strengths of those with whom they will be working. Operating from a strengths-based approach honors individual differences.

Sharing strengths is the first step in discovering the personal stories and experiences that have shaped an individual. It is through the sharing of stories that begins to lead to authentic conversation and vulnerability. I am sure that taking the time to learn about others on this level doesn't seem like important work in a school setting, but I would venture to say that not spending this time is the reason why many of our problems keep occurring year after year. Individuals will not be able to engage in productive conflict if they do not trust or feel safe in the environment in which they are working. Being vulnerable is about "having the courage to show up and be seen when we have no control over the outcome" of what others think about our ideas or us as individuals (Brene Brown). Knowing who we are and the strengths we bring to the table begins to peel back the layers that sometimes prevent us from sharing the best parts of ourselves.

Understanding The Way We Work

When I was an elementary principal, I led my staff through an activity that was designed to identify individual work styles. There are a number of work style assessments that can be found, but the one I am most familiar with is the Compass Points activity from the National School Reform Faculty. When my staff completed the profile, over 80% of the staff worked in a way that was the polar opposite of how I preferred to work as an individual and how I led as a leader. You can imagine the relief I felt in recognizing that the actions of the staff had nothing to do with them being difficult just for the sake of causing me grief, but it had everything to do with how they worked best and what they needed in order to be successful and feel supported to do their best work.

Understanding that we all work differently is important when trying to accomplish goals as a team. Often we can become frustrated when working with individuals who work differently than we do. For example, I am a quick processor and am able to make decisions and understand complex concepts rather quickly. Before I spent time learning about the different working styles, I would find myself getting frustrated when working with individuals who would ask a number of questions or struggle to make a decision. This type of working style would interrupt my flow, and I perceived it as an attempt to derail my ideas or challenge my perceptions. Recognizing that we all work and process differently helped me to respect the different styles, especially how those styles helped me to improve upon an idea and increase the productivity of the team.

Establishing Collective Agreements

A common exercise that occurs when a team forms is the development of group norms, which is the standard behavior that is expected of each group member. While norms are adequate enough for teams that may not work together for a lengthy time on a project, the exercise of establishing collective agreements are more appropriate for teams that will be engaging in meaningful work over a long course of time. Collective means that all team members have worked together to establish agreements that are rooted in individual core beliefs and values. Establishing these agreements requires more of a commitment at a deeper level. Instead of adopting a set of norms, it is important to consciously develop agreements collaboratively, post them visually, and reflect and revisit them often.

I can recall on many occasions when staff members would come to me with an issue they were having with a team member. After they shared their concern, I would ask them about the collective agreements they established. I thought it was important for me to remind them that at some point they worked together as a team to prepare for the moment they were currently experiencing. Establishing these agreements does nothing for the group

TABLE 6.1 Teaching Trust Leadership Teams Program

Destructive Responses	Productive Responses
Arguing	Apologizing
Sarcasm	Being willing to compromise
Dominating the conversation	Acknowledging others' feelings
Refusing to accept feedback	Listening to others perspectives
Blaming	Being flexible
Condescending	Separating emotions from facts
Giving in	Giving people time and space
Taking things personally	Stepping back to reflect
Embellishing the situation	Communicating openly and
Shutting down/Avoidance	honestly
Passive aggressive behavior	Accepting responsibility
Gossiping or complaining about someone	

if the agreements are not used for the intended purpose. Referring back to these agreements creates a safe environment for productive conflict to occur. Unproductive conflict is a result of allowing destructive responses to be the "rules of engagement" when conflict arises.

As individuals, we have this innate desire to make sure our needs are met and that we protect ourselves from harm. If a team did not take the time to establish agreements about how they will work together as a group, the moment that conflict arises the natural response will be to protect ourselves and our ideas. There is less work and effort involved when using destructive responses to address conflict; however, using productive responses to engage in productive conflict involves more work, discipline, courage and vulnerability. For example, having impromptu meetings to criticize ideas or teammates after a scheduled team meeting is counterproductive to the way of the high performing teams. This type of behavior is a direct threat to any high performing team.

Being committed to engage in a more productive way takes collective commitment, responsibility and accountability. When individuals are behaving outside of the collective agreements that have been established, it is the responsibility of the team to address this issue. My wise colleague, Onika Mayers, so candidly stated "relationships matter, people." If that statement is true, we will have the courage to hold each other accountable for making sure the team works within the agreements they established.

Preparing for the Wave of Conflict

Conflict is inevitable. Preparing for when the opportunity to engage in productive conflict comes is the easy part. Using the tools and strategies that you created and practiced when everything was harmonious is the challenge. Prior to each team meeting, it is important to review the collective agreements. These agreements need to be visible and read aloud by each member of the group. This puts the agreements into the space before the work begins. It is also important to remind the team of the collective agreements if the team begins to work outside of those agreements. Analyzing the current team dynamics by using structured protocols to guide discussion gives individuals time to reflect prior to sharing their thoughts with the group. This allows each person to have a voice and minimizes group think. Keeping the pulse on the dynamics of the team helps to fine tune trouble areas along the way. Think of it as a annual medical physical oil change, or AC maintenance. We all want our bodies, cars, and AC working at its best so preventive maintenance should be top priority. The dynamics of the team may be working for most members, but if the analysis is not unanimous, then it is imperative to resolve any issues that could be preventing an individual from doing their best work.

In the absence of knowledge, people create their own stories. When the expectations for the work of the group and the problem that needs to be solved have not been clearly identified or explicitly stated, individuals will create their own way of working. It is unfair to expect someone to meet expectations that have not been shared with them. Assuming that team members know the direction the team is going, or know the best way in which to complete the work, is foolish. This type of approach creates the expectation that individual work is preferred when really a group approach and product is the expected outcome. Unstated or unclear expectations are often the most fundamental reason for conflict. In order to engage productively, the expectations for the work must be shared and revisited often throughout the process.

Using Productive Conflict to Attack Adaptive Challenges

Many of the challenges that school teams face require engaging in productive conflict. In the book, *Leadership on the Line* (2002), Heifetz defines two types of challenges. "Technical challenges can be defined as those that can be solved by the knowledge of the experts, whereas adaptive challenges requires new learning." Issues such as scheduling recess and lunch, increasing efficiency in the car rider line, or creating the master schedule are technical challenges. The solution to these issues is clear and does not require changes that have a significant impact over time.

Technical challenges usually can be solved without engaging in productive conflict because they are clear cut and don't involve a great deal of emotional connection to the decision. On the other hand, issues that challenge the philosophies and fundamental thoughts of individuals, such as assessment practices, social justice, social and emotional learning, race and culture, etc. are adaptive challenges that require a new way of learning. These issues can be personal to individuals and are usually rooted in the their perspective and experiences.

Many of the fundamental practices that we do in schools across the country have remained the same, and it is my belief that our inability to peel away at the issues by engaging in productive conflict instead of taking sides has created this barrier to breaking free of what we have always done. In schools, there are challenges that continue to arise each year. The reason these challenges have not been solved is because individuals have not figured out a way to relax their stance on an issue so that teams can look at each idea and use those ideas as a catalyst to create the best idea together. Engaging in productive conflict creates a pathway to creativity. Individuals who are committed to finding novel solutions always believe there is a better way and that their idea is only one piece of the puzzle.

Handling Conflict in the Middle of a Storm

Imagine a team meeting where one team member usually dominates the conversation. This team member is more outspoken, opinionated and freely shares ideas that they expect others to implement. On the same team is a member who is quiet and does not feel comfortable sharing ideas for fear that his or her ideas may be rejected. Although this individual has some great ideas that have been successful, the thought of sharing is perceived as speaking out or disagreeing with the outspoken colleague. To round out the team, there is a teammate who tries to remain neutral. Neutrality works because it doesn't force the person to take sides. At the same time, the neutral teammate fears that sharing a different perspective or approach will cause the dominant team member to form an alliance with the quiet team member so that the only idea that will be considered is the one shared by the dominant team member. Does this sound familiar?

Scenarios like the one mentioned above are so prevalent in our schools today. No wonder we are still trying to solve the same issues year after year. In Lencioni's work, *The Five Dysfunctions of a Team* (2002), the fear of conflict is one of the five dysfunctions the author shares. This fear of conflict is developed because of the lack of trust between team members. Individuals who are committed to the I, me, my, mine thought process or find strength in dominance are creating environments that stifle productive conflict and perpetuate inequitable working environments. Those who can put we before me and focus on the collectiveness of the group create environments where all voices are heard and all ideas are respected.

As a leader, I **handle** unproductive conflict on a regular basis. I bolded the word handle because this is exactly what must happen when unproductive conflict arises. To ignore conflict actually gives the conflict power. Now don't get me wrong, I am not a conflict seeker, but I do seek to resolve and address conflict so that all parties mutually agree with the outcome.

When dealing with conflict between teachers, I always ask each party how I can help. Many times one teacher will come into my office to share their displeasure about another colleague. Even if I have an opinion about the issue or the colleague, I never share it. My job is to listen and not to discredit the individual or add fuel to the flame. I ask the person the following question when they finish giving me the details of the conflict, "What was the response when you told your colleague how you felt?" The reaction I usually get is one of shock. They usually respond by telling me that they haven't talked to the person, and in most cases, they have no intention of doing so. Most people don't address the conflict head on. They are looking for a solution to the conflict that does not involve the person directly involved in the conflict.

Your leadership style will determine how you assist others. If you are a manager, you quickly give them ways you would address the issue and wish them luck on coming to a resolution.

If you are a leader, you help them devise a plan that includes strategies they can use to resolve not only the current conflict but conflicts that may arise in the future. Then you follow up with them to see if the plan worked and determine if they need to revise or change their approach. The manager resolves issues quickly by putting a bandaid on the problem while the leader repairs harm and heals relationships.

When I experience a conflict with a teacher, I pull back from the situation and assess my actions and emotions. The easy fix to a principal-teacher conflict is to assert my authority as the principal to resolve the conflict on my terms; however, in my opinion, the best way to solve the conflict is to listen, seek to understand, acknowledge wrongdoing, whether it is perceived on intentional, and work to repair the relationship.

Leaders need to seek to make things right at all times. We don't always have to be right or get the final word. We can't take responsibility for someone else's emotions but we can certainly take ownership for our own actions. Always assume the best intentions from people. This is not easy, but it is so worth it. Leaders should be problem-solvers, conflict-resolvers, and relationship builders. This triple threat equips leaders with the skills to handle any conflicts that may come their way.

Resolving Conflict Productively

At the end of the day, I don't think people desire to be conflict warriors. Most individuals do not seek to work in situations where unproductive conflict is the norm. However, expecting productive conflict and equipping yourself with strategies to navigate the conflict successfully is the difference between good teams and great teams. Consider the following strategies as you prepare to create spaces that promote and encourage productive conflict.

Become Self-Aware
Before being able to fully engage in productive conflict, having a strong sense of self-awareness is key. Individuals who can acknowledge, describe and understand their own feelings,

while comprehending how their personal feelings and behaviors impact others have a strong sense of self. Engaging in personal reflection helps one to get to this level. Once you have a strong sense of self, you are more apt to perceive and understand the perspective of others. Spend some time journaling and responding to reflective questions. Be honest with yourself about how you are feeling about situations. If you can't be honest with yourself, you will not be equipped to engage in honest sharing and reflecting with others.

Be Open to Feedback

Personal reflection is like looking in the mirror and identifying every beauty mark, blemish, wrinkle and scar. Reflecting should make us feel raw and exposed, but the thought of being receptive to feedback should make us feel courageous. If we truly want to grow as individuals and educators, we must practice courage over comfort. We cannot have both (Brown, 2015). As we strive to grow, refine, and reshape ourselves as educators, we shouldn't look for the people who are going to praise us or our work all of the time. We should seek out the ones who will be honest with us, and we must be willing to accept their feedback.

Practice Active Listening

Have you ever wondered why we have two ears and one mouth? Hearing is activity that requires little thought or effort, but active listening is a skill that must be practiced. Our first inclination is to hear so that we can respond. When we engage in a hearing exercise, we are only focused on hearing so that we can respond. In order be fully engaged when someone is speaking, we must listen more than we intend to speak. Instead of interjecting our response or thoughts, we should repeat what we heard the person staying. Using statements such as "What I hear your saying is . . ." or "Help me to understand how you got to this conclusion" are useful statements that support active listening. It is important to ask questions when seeking clarity instead of trying to make sense of the gaps through our own lens. Active listening requires writing, thinking, and processing, but it does not require an immediate response.

Engage in Courageous Conversations

Educators tend to shy away from engaging in tough conversations. Especially in our current day and age when it seems we are constantly being attacked by the public. The last thing we want to do is engage in emotionally charged conversations with our colleagues. However, what if not engaging in courageous conversations is perpetuating the behaviors and ideas we are so often criticized for by others outside of our industry? Would you want to know how to be better? Others outside of our profession have no reservations about sharing their voice about how we, the experts, should be conducting our business as educators. It is time for us to share our voice and ideas with each other so that we can eliminate groupthink and the echo chambers that have unintentionally been created because of our fear of engaging in productive conflict.

Bringing it All Together

When engaging in productive conflict there is no right and wrong – only different. Being able to see someone else's perspective for what it is rather than through the filter of what you think it should be is the first critical step. Productive conflict does not occur by appealing to the logical part of the brain. If you want anyone to change, it is a must that you appeal to the emotional side of the brain first. Emotionally intelligent individuals practice self and social awareness and are strategic in managing relationships. They have the ability to control their emotions and understand the effect their attitude and actions have on others, which enables them to adapt their behavior to elicit positive and productive outcomes.

People need to feel and connect before they are able to change. True connection cannot happen in the absence of true relationship building. Authenticity will not grow if planted in inauthentic soil. As Peter Senge simply states, "In great teams, conflict becomes productive. The free flow of conflicting ideas is critical for creative thinking, for discovering new solutions no one individual would have come to on his own" (Brent & Dent, 2017).

If doing the work that is required to cultivate high-performing teams is important to you, you will find the time and create the space; if it is not, you will find an excuse. The role of the leader is not to have all the answers to the many challenges we face. The role of the leader is to create an environment in which all ideas are shared, valued, respected and appreciated. Take the time to do the culture work that is necessary to create environments where productive conflict can thrive, for it is the strength of the team's culture that will determine the altitude of the group.

References

Brent, M. & Dent, F. (2017). *The leadership of teams: How to develop and inspire high-performance teamwork.* New York: Bloomsbury Publishing.

Brown, B. (2015). *Rising strong: The reckoning. The rumble. The revolution.* New York: Random House Books.

Heifetz, R. & Linsky, M. (2002) *Leadership on the line: Staying alive through the dangers of change.* Boston: Harvard Business Review Press.

HuffPost. www.huffingtonpost.com/amy-brann/the-neuroscience-of-emotional-intelligence_b_9331292.html.

Lencioni, P. (2002). *The five dysfunctions of a team: A leadership fable.* San Francisco: Jossey Bass.

National School Reform Faculty. www.nsrfharmony.org/.

Teaching Trust (2018). *Engaging in productive conflict.* Raise Your Hand Texas Leadership Symposium. Houston, TX.

7

Connecting Beyond the Four Walls

Onica L. Mayers

Know Your Why

Two years ago, as I embarked upon my fourth year as an elementary school principal, I still believed in that age-old adage . . . it's lonely at the top. When you hear something repeatedly it seeps into your psyche and you begin to believe it's true. Fast forward to today, that phrase is no longer part of my belief system. In fact, what I know to be true is that it can be lonely at the top or any other rung on the ladder . . . but only if you want it to be. Choosing to be isolated on an island as an educator – principal, teacher, counselor, director, instructional coach, superintendent – is just that – a choice. We all have the power to choose whether we work in silos, or go beyond the four walls to become connected to those who can elevate our thinking.

During a typical Sunday evening conversation with my husband, I began mapping out the week ahead while scrolling through my Twitter feed. At the time, I was encouraging the teachers on my campus to share our school's story through Twitter, and also found that it was an increasingly resourceful professional learning opportunity for me. I came across a tweet from Lindsy Stumpenhorst (@principalboots) where she shared – There are moms. There are principals. Then there are the crazy ones who do both. My husband didn't see the big deal when I exclaimed that there are other crazies like me out there in the world – Moms as Principals. I visited the blog post linked to the tweet and remembered thinking . . . these people are speaking my language. There was an immediate sense of connection. I felt a sense of belonging that I had not felt in my then 17 years of education. I was instantly comfortable being my authentic self.

Connection is important! According to *Psychology Today*, one of our fundamental needs as human beings is that sense of social connection. In essence, connections help to build personal and professional relationships that lead to a deeper awareness of our true selves. By connecting with those beyond one's immediate circle of influence, we:

- ◆ feed our emotional intelligence desires;
- ◆ gain knowledge from others through discovery;
- ◆ share our own learning and feel a sense of contributing to the greater good, and
- ◆ become more energized and inspired to continue doing the work we are committed to.

Feeding Your Emotional Intelligence

After connecting with Moms as Principals on Twitter, I asked to be a member of their Voxer group. I recall driving to work that first morning after joining the group. I listened to a few voxes, caught the rhythm of how others shared and responded, and mustered the courage to send my first vox. And I know what you're thinking, "You were hesitant about speaking into a phone with people who had no idea who you were?" Yes . . . although I spoke with hundreds of students daily and more than 120 staff members, fear of that unknown had me unsettled. In education, we often hear failure is not an option. What if we changed that mindset to failure is an option? What if we believed failure is the only option? By being willing to fail, we are demonstrating a willingness to learn and grow, and isn't that what we ultimately want from students?

So eventually I pressed the orange Voxer button, "Good morning MAPS. This is Onica Mayers from Houston checking in. I'm the principal of a PK – 5th grade campus in Houston, Texas." I shared a few details about my campus, thanked them for allowing me to be a part of their learning network and shared that I was looking forward to learning and growing from and with them. I kept my introductory message short and sweet, cognizant of the established norms which included keeping your vox under a minute. That was the genesis of it all. To begin, begin. I cannot even imagine my professional and personal life now without this tribe.

That morning, I wanted to pull over to write down the many ideas that others were sharing. The conversations were rich and diverse; when one member asked about suggestions for revamping her Response to Intervention (RtI) process, within minutes there were at least four ideas offered. Another member came on and asked everyone to keep a staff member in prayer because the teacher's daughter was diagnosed with a terminal illness. I thought . . . goodness . . . this is deep. What I didn't realize at the time, but certainly recognize two years later, was that prior to connecting with this group, I failed to feed my emotional intelligence as an educator and more importantly as a leader. Thus, I was not capable of feeding the emotional intelligence of those I served and I had the audacity to wonder why the culture of the campus wasn't what I hoped for. In education, we are fortunate that every day is the opportunity to turn over a new leaf and through my new-found connections, my decision-making process became more inclusive.

The Institute of Health and Human Potential defines emotional intelligence as an awareness that emotions can drive our behavior which has both a positive and negative impact on people. In education, we are in the people business, be it the little people (students) or the big people (adult learners). If you want to consider yourself emotionally intelligent then you have to work consciously on your emotional skills if you are going to have the positive impact on either targeted audience. In my very first educational leadership class, we read *If You Don't Feed the Teachers They Eat the Students*. What happens if you don't feed the leaders? Who do they eat? Feeding one's emotional intelligence as a leader is essential to the success of whomever you serve. If you are a teacher, you are a leader of students, if you are a campus leader, well, it goes without saying that you are leading students, staff, parents and community members. If you are an instructional coach, you are leading teachers. When your emotional intelligence is not fed, how can you feed others?

Undoubtedly, students learn better in safe and supportive learning environments, and the same can be said for adults. By connecting with a group of like-minded individuals, I found myself better equipped to handle the day-to-day situations and struggles as a leader. By having a support system, a network to reach out to with those who "get it," I found myself better able to navigate the current educational terrain. This connection is not just to help with the struggles but also to celebrate the successes. We call them #EduWins and in order to elevate your class, campus, department or district towards whatever your desired outcomes are, genuine connections are a prerequisite, and that requires a high emotional intelligence. You must put yourself first on this emotional intelligence journey.

   ◆ Know Yourself – clearly seeing what you feel and do, reflecting on your strengths and challenges, and recognizing your behavior patterns.
   ◆ Choose Yourself – proactively responding to situations instead of reacting as if on autopilot.
   ◆ Give Yourself – putting your vision into action, knowing your purpose, and doing things with intentionality.

When you have a tribe, it's like having your personal cheerleaders behind you every step of the way. Knowing that you have an outlet strengthens you. Think about why we have counselors in schools for students. Students have their teachers they can turn to, yet the counselor serves as that non-threatening avenue for students to be able to reach out and get the support needed. We, as educators, need the same, if not more support from someone, or people, who are not going to judge us, who are sometimes there to simply listen, yet other times share that one AHA that puts your emotions in check when our brains are under pressure. When you can connect your emotions to others, you in turn can engage, inspire and motivate those who are depending on you to feed their emotional intelligence. It supports an open and growth mindset that leads to knowledge discovery.

Knowledge Discovery

My 11-year-old son is a typical pre-teen. He will spend hours playing his Xbox Live if only we would let him. With the laundry basket in hand, I rounded the corner from my bedroom to the living room and I could hear him speaking to someone, and silly me thought he was engaged in a conversation with one of his two brothers. To my utter surprise, he was indeed engrossed in a conversation, but not with anyone in our home. He had just received a set of headphones for his birthday and they were his new BFF. This one simple tool allowed him to connect beyond the four walls of our home. There he was, strategizing his next move with his friend who lived in a totally different subdivision. I listened in as he shared his plan, his friend offered up a better suggestion, he altered his plan, he added to what was shared, he rejoiced when it worked, and they kept it moving. Kids willingly connect because they see the benefit in it for them. They don't keep their learning tucked away in a box . . . unwilling to share or seek out new ways of doing from others.

Over dinner that evening, I asked about his shared experience with what I thought was between him and one other friend. I quickly learned that it was not one, but four other friends playing together – his tribe. Your vibe attracts your tribe, so why aren't we seeing the benefits in connecting beyond our four walls? Today's 11-year-olds are so much smarter than we think. They recognized that through connecting with others with similar interests and desires (to win the game), they refined their original ways of doing, abandoned what was not working, gained new insight, and by sharing with others deepened their own craft and level of expertise.

Today, there is simply no excuse as to why we are not connecting beyond our immediate four walls. This is not to say that there is anything wrong with connecting within your current walls; by all means, that should be a given. My son had played this same game with his two brothers at home many times before, but because they played together all the time, their learning scope was limited. None of them had "new knowledge" to bring to the table. Now collaborating with others, he was learning new methodologies that he could use when playing with his brothers, thus making him more successful in his approach to the game, and helping them to get better at their craft as well. Connections became the vehicle for the domino effect of success for all involved.

In each of my roles, I was connected with those I was in physical contact with daily. I had personal and professional connections. I could share ideas and ask questions, but when I think back to all of my firsts – first year as teacher, instructional coach, assistant principal, principal - they were filled with failures and pitfalls; some could have been avoided had I been a connected educator. Within the walls, we were all doing the same thing, and doing it the way we've always done it. It wasn't that there wasn't a growth mindset; the growth was limited because of the limitations we each had. That is the key to connecting beyond the walls, others do things differently, often making you think, "Why didn't I think of that before?"

After my first year teaching, clearly flying by the seat of my pants on many, many days, I realized that I had failed one student. I could say I failed more than one, but I definitely failed one, Cynthia. She was a shy fourth grader who I would now describe as compliant, she knew how to "do school." She was present daily, appeared attentive (I now know that she was not engaged), and did what was required. She was not on my radar, not until it was too late. When her New York State fourth grade reading language arts results came back, she did not meet the standard. How did that happen? I hadn't seen that coming not even from a mile away. I had met with my grade-level colleagues weekly for team planning. We looked at data, described our students, strategized our next steps, but no one, myself included, ever saw Cynthia as a student who could possibly fail. I now think about all the what ifs. What if another teacher, perhaps in a different district or state had described a student like Cynthia who they noticed was struggling? Could that have enlightened me to the fact that I had a similar student who was failing right before my eyes? Could I have gotten ideas on recognizing compliance versus engagement? As an instructional coach, I was responsible for setting teachers up for instructional success. This was the role where really, I didn't know what I didn't know. When teachers came to me with questions, I delved into books and sought support with online resources, but didn't have another instructional coach to reach out to. I was grabbing at straws and needed a lifeline but didn't know where to look although surely someone was out there to save me. I did the best that I could, but I think now about the authentic feedback I could have given if I had the knowledge base to do so. I was a fixer of all things instructional versus a facilitator who empowered teachers to learn by doing. I know now, many years later, that I needed to be connected myself in order to best help those I served.

The past 14 years of my career has been in administrative capacities. During that span of time, I know that I failed students, teachers, parents and community members. I know that continuing to fail is a part of life's process of growth, but we can fail forward when we are connected. The connections that will work are those you truly care about. As educators, it is imperative that we identify what we have a genuine interest in and use that as the starting line for making connections. Commit to seeking out information and begin to actively pay attention to those who share that passion. We have to be willing to invest the time if it truly matters. It is evident that we cannot leave connections to chance.

As we prepare our students to be digital natives, we can take advantage of all the tools accessible to us as educators to not only connect with others but to stay connected. I agree with Dr. Winston Sakurai, NASSP National Digital Principal, when he says that social media is not just for keeping up with the Kardashians. Move beyond your four walls via:

◆ Twitter – I initially identified my influencers, people whose work I previously read which impacted me as an educator. Find a few people who seem to have similar interests in education and follow them. You can even send that person a direct message (DM) if you are interested in more information about something he/she tweeted out. I stepped out on a limb last year and started the first edCamp in our district. I reached out to numerous authors through direct message and they all sent autographed copies of their texts as door prizes. I couldn't believe how impactful Twitter connections were. Follow a few hashtags of interest (#EdWriteNow, #KidsDeserveIt, #TLAP, #LeadLap, #Edchat, #LEAPeffect, #LeadUpChat – to name a few) and scroll through the feed. Take one idea per week and try it out. It's guaranteed to be a game changer. Consider participating in a Twitter chat (and it's okay to be a Twitter chat stalker at first, but to truly connect, you must move from stalking to participating).

◆ Voxer – This walkie talkie app is used to connect people personally and professionally. The first group I joined was Moms as Principals and later Principals in Action. Two years in, Voxer has become my coffee in the morning (and I don't drink coffee but checking in with my groups en route to work each morning is my morning energizer), and it's my Dr. Pepper on my ride home in the evening (and I don't drink Dr. Pepper but it's what helps me to reflect on the day by listening and learning from others). There are hundreds of Voxer groups. You can participate in book studies and even create your own Voxer chats. The next time you attend a professional development session, ask two or three others serving in a similar capacity to start a Voxer chat with you. You will become each other's accountability partners and develop such a collaborative spirit that you'll wonder how you survived without it. A simple search for www.cybraryman.com/

voxer.html will give you more groups than you will ever need to be connected beyond your four walls.

◆ Blogs – There are the times when you need to read a full-length book to deepen your understanding of a concept, and there are opportunities for learning that can happen in snapshots a few minutes at a time. That's when subscribing to blogs come in ever so handy. Blogs are written to capture the essence of a specific topic. A few of my favorite go-to reads that sharpen my skill set are: Cool Cat Teacher, The Principal of Change, The @DavidGuerin Blog, Moms as Principals, Teacher Tech with Alice Keeler, A Principal's Reflections, Ignite a Culture of Innovation, Pernille Ripp, The Principal Blog. I dare you to leave a comment and get connected with the author.

◆ Podcasts – What's your commute like? The reality is that most of us commute to work daily, so think about how you use that time. Welcome – Podcast PD, or as Danny Sunshine Bauer calls it, Commuting University. As a committed learner, you can leverage the time you spend in traffic, walking on the treadmill, or doing the laundry by listening to what inspires you and feeds your soul. Get your phone, sit by your computer, grab your headphones, and begin by finding a trusted "voice" that shapes your educational focus today. Repurpose your time by using ITunes, YouTube or Google as search engines to discover new knowledge. If you want to listen to an expert share about the benefit on restorative practices in supporting building relationships with students, then search just that. Other great podcasts to help you connect beyond your four walls (these are just a few to get you started, the list is endless) – Better Leaders Better Schools, The Cult of Pedagogy, Transformative Principal with Jethro Jones, Angela Watson's Truth for Teachers, Every Classroom Matters, Principal Center Radio. Which one will you commit to subscribing to? Just start with one and begin to connect the dots.

Connecting virtually requires a simple swipe or touch of a screen, however, do not underestimate the value in face-to-face connections which are empowering in breaking down the walls of learning. Seek out conferences that fuel your fire and make connections while there. Recently, I met face-to-face for the first time with a principal from Vero Beach, Florida. Cindy and I connected virtually and have been connected for two years. We are part of the same tribe on Voxer. We follow each other on Twitter. We've co-authored a blog post together and were there for each other during some trying times we each faced during the school year. We knew each other by voice and finally connected face-to-face. That initial meeting was epic! We had dinner and spent hours talking about everything from our families to the initiatives we were going to focus on for the upcoming school year and the "how" that would get us to our goals. We each walked away with a treasure chest of nuggets that was going to deepen our practice as leaders and the ultimate beneficiaries would be our school communities – our students. Our connection exemplified the Latin proverb, *By learning you will teach, by teaching you will learn.* When you share, you learn and ultimately contribute to the greater good of all students everywhere. After all, all kids are our kids!

Learning and Contributing

No one is exempt. Even the biggest and most influential people in the world have something they'd like help with. If asked, I can certainly raise both hands and say yes, I'm guilty of not wanting to reach out to others thinking I have nothing to offer in return. What we don't recognize is that we have more to offer if we would fully immerse ourselves and be vulnerable when sharing our own our learning. In sharing, there is a sense of celebration and members of the school community, district, department, and/or organization, begin to feel more connected.

Begin by sharing your successes and then your struggles. I wanted our teachers to share their learning with each other and begin to seek out others who could support their learning as well, knowing that it would help to create an atmosphere of collegiality where students ultimately thrive. As I visited classes daily, I felt proud of the instruction that unfolded before my eyes. It was a great learning environment for students; one that I would gladly place my three personal children in.

But with more than 70 teachers and 30 support staff members on a campus, how could they possibly learn from others outside of their immediate grade level or content team when they do not all share common planning times? Knowing that teachers do not have extended periods of time on their hands, and thinking of myself as a learner, one who does not like to sit in long, drawn out learning sessions, I wondered how we could support each other in chunks. I went back to the notes I had taken a few months prior at the annual TCEA (Texas Computer Education Association) conference and came across a "thought-bubble" I had written down for future use. It was an appropriate time to share the idea of creating *Bite-Size PD* on our campus. As we approached the midpoint of the school year, I posted the following in my weekly Mayers Minutes communication to the staff:

Curriculum and Instruction News

Bitesize PD – Do you have an idea, teaching/strategy tip or technology tool that you would like to share? Bitesize PD is coming this spring. We're looking for teachers who want to facilitate learning conversations from 4:15–4:30 PM (yes, only 15 minutes of PD). This is a great opportunity to share something you've learned or are trying out in your classroom that you think others can benefit from. If interested, please sign up for the day you want to share and indicate the topic on the document posted outside my office on Monday. Those presenting will receive 1-hour off-contact PD time (15 minutes to share and 45 minutes credit for planning the session) and those who attend 4 (15-minute) sessions this spring will receive 1-hour PD credit.

Do you know how much learning can take place in 15 minutes? You'd be surprised. As I heard teachers talking about it, they were relieved that if they wanted to share with their colleagues, the sessions would only be 15 minutes, and they could host them in their classrooms. Eventually some asked if they could do their sessions before school instead of after – absolutely! I was just elated that the concept had captured their interest. Our *Bite-Size PD* series took off, and before we knew it, the learning was infectious. Teachers were sharing about plans to support blended learning, collaborating on BreakOut EDU lessons, offering class-room organization tips, intervention strategies for ELLS, provid-ing brain boosts to make the learning stick, managing guided reading groups, you name it. The 15 minutes was enough to wet their appetites, give them something to go back and try out, and have a go-to person if they needed to follow up. Connections were being made beyond their four walls – beyond their grade level or content teams. It was powerful to see kindergarten and fifth grade teachers sharing concepts. The teachers posted their learning and the ideas they were trying out on Twitter, they were transparent in asking for feedback or additional suggestions, and no one claimed to be "an expert." They were simply sharing and ultimately learning more through the process. They were stunned when teachers from within the district, across the state and throughout the country started making connections with them asking them to elaborate on some of their ideas. As they shared, they began to collect more knowledge as well. They were contributing to the greater good of students beyond their four walls and now were connected educators themselves.

I remember when one teacher came by and shared that the 15 minutes was great, but she used a new app, wanted to share how her students benefited, but it would take more than 15 minutes to share the what and the how with others. "Would 30 minutes work?" I asked. With that, we added 30-minute ses-sions – PD Lite, and for those who needed 45 minutes, we called those Share Sessions. All were totally voluntary on the part of those who shared and those who attended. We had instructional coaches on our campus, but it was empowering to seeing our classroom teachers leading the way. In sharing with each other, they were teaching others, and digging deeper to get better at their pedagogy as well. That's how our #EachOneTeachOne series was born. The majority of the staff felt that the 30-minute sessions would be sufficient to capture the essence of what they wanted to share. After reflecting and seeking input, we now offer three 30-minute sessions monthly and teachers have the option to attend a session that most meets their learning needs. The sessions are videotaped and archived in our online resource library, so that teachers who didn't have an opportunity to attend a session, can always go back and see what was shared. New teachers to our campus will also have that resource available to them so that they can begin to make their own connections.

We connected the dots of learning across the campus and beyond our walls and now operate in a different system of norms, values and beliefs. The way "we do things around here" change when you are surrounded by like-minded people pushing you to know better, and when you know better, you do better. Believe in the power and purpose of connecting, learning and sharing. Connect the dots outside your four walls by writing an article or blog post. In your post you may not feel like you have enough to share, but what about a post reaching out for support with something you're struggling with in your respective area of content/ expertise? Share it with those you connect with. Take the time to give real thought to who you could connect with to benefit your goals and theirs. In one of Jimmy Casas' Thought of the Day via *Culturize* – he notes, "Four of the most powerful words for educators and students to use if they want to be successful – I Need Your Help. Alone we can be an example, together we can be an exemplar." Through connectedness there is self enhancement, possibilities are expanded and everyone is inspired and committed to continuing the work to support students. In fact, when you share with others, the sense of validation for your efforts contributes to the greater good of those who serve as it helps to energize and inspire you to continue your gift of service.

Energy and Inspiration

Think for a moment about the last time you were in a space when someone received a standing ovation. How did that begin? It started because one person clapped. Then another, another, and another. In only a few seconds, the whole room was clapping and then one person stood, another, and another. Everyone was then on their feet. You could feel the energy in that space and everyone feels connected. You may have left feeling inspired. Did you do something with that inspiration? It starts with one, and that one could be you. Educators are difference makers and difference makers cannot do this work alone. In connecting beyond the four walls, you begin to get your ideas validated by those who may not necessarily share the same ideas, but the same desires to do something great. As human beings, we have an insatiable need for acceptance from our peers.

There are nine of us on my campus-based leadership team. We meet weekly, if not daily at times, and are immersed in a collaborative environment. Even in that supportive space, I knew I needed more. You "catch" energy from interacting with others walking the same path. As the campus leader, you sit in a unique role, and there's only one you. Interestingly, I attended our monthly principal meetings and was collegial with all my peers, but it wasn't until a deeper connection was made with two of them that I felt propelled to a different level of engagement as a leader. I had known Kelly and Cathy for two years. We would wave at meetings, share smiles, and occasionally bounce an idea off each other. Then they both joined a Voxer group that I was in when I shared the impact that it was having on my daily work. I would hear them as they collaborated in this national group of principals, and thought, *our schools are in the same district and I never knew this or that about what they were doing*. We were crafting like-minded initiatives, supporting similar demographics of students, and experiencing the same concerns, yet we weren't connecting each other's dots. The three of us recognized this and started collaborating almost daily. I was now connecting with those who "got it" and felt that while I may have been in my office solo, I was not alone on the journey. There was less isolation working together, more accountability amongst us, a safe space and ability to share ideas, and more importantly, I was having fun with my peers. We have since visited each other's campuses, worked on plans together, and have connected staff members to collaborate and see the value in connecting beyond our four walls. When you feel like you can't, others will help you to figure out how you can. Building high-quality connections and strengthening social capital is a sure way to improve as an educator.

I found that the teachers on my campus were inspiring and energizing other educators beyond our four walls. As I saw the greatness in them, I gave simple nods and pushes for them to step out of their comfort zone and present at local conferences. Recognizing that I needed to model what I was suggesting they do, I reached out to my learning tribe to get feedback on my first presentation. I sent messages to principals across the country, almost all of whom I never met face-to-face, and shared the concepts that were formulating in my mind for the topic that I was going to present on. They generously shared their thoughts and feedback and I in turn fed off of their energy. It was the momentum I needed to confidently walk into my first presentation feeling their belief and presence with me. I was so immensely grateful to them and that gratitude for the help received encourages me to pay it forward and continue helping and serving others.

If you somehow feel that you're sitting in an energy crisis, you can do something about it. The more you energize those around you, the more you will feel inspired to continue doing the work to which you are committed. Focus on relational energy, that energy we get from interacting with others. Surround yourself with those who lift your spirits. Again, your vibe attracts your tribe. Getting help from others is simply one part of the multi-faceted puzzle we face daily. We also need to be able to validate, support, and help ourselves. Get in the habit of asking yourself, "What do I need right now?" Then seek it out from those with whom you connect. Contribute meaningfully to those you are connecting with and they will want to tap into your potential. In the end, Charles Bukowski says it best, "What matters most is how well you walk through the fire." Know that you need not walk through the fire alone. Relationships matter, people! Go connect beyond your four walls.

Resources

Casas, J. (2017). *Culturize: Every student. Every day. Whatever it takes.* San Diego: Dave Burgess Consulting, Inc.

https://momsasprincipals.wordpress.com/2016/09/06/keep-calm-and-mother-on/.

https://medium.com/thrive-global/the-softer-side-why-making-personal-connections-is-important-for-your-business-and-career-ed6711cbdb6e.

www.psychologytoday.com/us/blog/feeling-it/201208/connect-thrive.

www.ihhp.com/meaning-of-emotional-intelligence.

https://hbr.org/2016/09/the-energy-you-give-off-at-work-matters.

www.edutopia.org/blog/developing-teachers-social-emotional-skills-lorea-martinez.

8

Connecting Through the Power of Generosity

Winston Sakurai

Kindness and generosity can transform people's lives. Do you agree? I hope you do. It is a positivity that can uplift spirits, motivate students and propel schools forward. More importantly it can bind individuals together in tightly woven ways though a personal circumstance. Think about the last time someone was generous with their time, talent or resources with you. What emotions were stirred up after receiving that thoughtful gift? How was it helpful to you? Now think about something that you did to support someone else. How did being generous make you feel? What you will find is that there is an emotional transaction that takes place between individuals that brings them closer together. So why does this happen? It is because humans have the capacity and an innate desire to be generous. It is important to us because generous educators influence generous students who create a better and more generous world.

The University of Notre Dame Science of Generosity Initiative

The website https://generosityresearch.nd.edu/news/what-makes-us-generous/ looks at different approaches from philanthropy to volunteerism to altruism, finding these themes important enough to combine them into a unique field of study. They define generosity simply as, "the virtue of giving good things to others freely and abundantly." Their research shows what most of us suspect. Those who are generous are happier, live healthier lives and have a purpose to life. Who wouldn't want those things? These are probably among some of the many reasons why people are so generous. So how do we cultivate generosity in our schools when we have so many other initiatives to deal with? The good news is that generosity can be learned through modeling and that is where we as educators do our best work. There is so much an educator can give. Most of it doesn't cost anything monetarily because we are good at giving of ourselves. Think about your own personal currency and see how you can convert that into impactful positive action.

Generosity is Learned

My parents were very generous people. They gave until it hurt, then they gave some more. Having generosity modeled for me throughout my life allowed me to be able to not only see what generosity looked like, but for it to be normalized. They both learned to be generous from their parents who were also known for their generosity. When my father passed away I was amazed at how many friends came up to share how he had personally helped them. Whether fixing a sink, or helping with car rides, or being generous with possessions he had offered his generosity. It makes you realize it's all about relationships people.

Living in Hawaii, there is also a culture of care that many refer to as the "Aloha Spirit". There are many ways that this type of giving of oneself is woven into the fabric of the people. For example, it is customary to have abundant amounts of food at any gathering so that people not only have enough to eat but also enough to take food home with them. Another ritual is to either bring or bring back little gifts when going on trips to give to family, coworkers and friends. Drivers in Hawaii typically allow others enough room to merge into traffic and commonly wave others to go ahead in front of them. It isn't uncommon for the other person to acknowledge the courtesy by waving back or by signing in gratitude with a shaka (a closed fist with a pinky and thumb extended). There is even a term for this: driving with aloha. Smiling and striking up conversations with strangers are also the norm. Although Hawaii may seem like a paradise in an isolated location, I believe the culture of generosity can be expressed and learned anywhere.

There are some warnings to those being kind and compassionate. Encountering others who are not accustomed to a culture of generosity sometimes provokes feelings of mistrust as to the intent. There have also been nefarious misuses of giving by people with ill intent. I mean how many times has a prince of a foreign country said he would share part of his trust fund with you if you send your bank information? Although generosity can sometimes be met with a healthy dose of skepticism and cynicism, wouldn't it be great if we lived in a culture that generously accepted generosity? They boil generosity down to its true meaning to be "good" and "free" and "abundant".

"Good" generosity should be something that truly meets a need and has the virtue of being good. There should be no Trojan horse giving. Nothing that looks likes a gift but is meant to hurt the person in the end for personal gain. For generosity to be good, it needs to not only be thought of as good by the giver, but also be understood as good by the recipient. Good generosity meets one or multiple needs of the recipient and is not a burden to receive.

"Free" generosity should not only come without a monetary cost, but also without the expectation of any form of reciprocity or quid pro quo. One shouldn't give with the expectation to be paid back in some form. There is a genuine nature to generosity that needs to exist. It is easy to identify when someone is not being sincere. Give freely.

"Abundant" generosity should meet the need beyond antici-pated. It could be overflowing and maybe even overwhelming. Think of it like a bountiful thanksgiving feast where there are succulent dishes galore. Give what you can give, but at the same time don't feel like you cannot give if you just have a little. Often times people don't cook the whole meal themselves. People bring different side dishes, desserts and other items. A little goes a long way, especially when it is combined with other gifts creating abundance for the receiver.

Generosity is Empathetic

Emotional generosity is the epitome of love that humans can show. Seeing a need and fulfilling that need. Educators must have a keen understanding of individuals and make a personal investment in working to help them to be successful. In short, they must care for others and be empathetic. When there is a need, time must be spent, the time to empathize, reflect upon how best to support, then make wise decisions that benefit both the school and individual. Schools likewise need to establish authentic opportunities for students to empathize with others.

Generosity is hospitality in its best form. It goes beyond being hospitable and a feeling of welcome from the recipient. It is an outpouring of yourself into the lives of others in some way, shape or form. It is filling a need whether tangible or intangible, spoken or unspoken, that you have the ability to fill. Doing so requires the ability to anticipate the needs of oth-ers and the ability to fulfill that need. True generosity requires empathy. The ability to see beyond and listen to what people are really saying and feeling and being able to draw out their true need is the first step. The second step that is required in true generosity is knowing what it will take to fulfill that need. The third and most crucial step is the action of generosity where it takes on an actionable form.

Educators are in a prime position to be able to change the lives of many through generosity. Think of all of the people in your circles of influence and everyone you encounter throughout the day. Those in leadership positions have large platforms to influence through generosity. Legislators, school board members, superintendents, principals, parents, grandparents, other family members, parent-teacher organization leaders, teachers, students and anyone in your community, the list is endless as to who can benefit from this spirit of generosity. In addition, leveraging social media to broaden that reach of influence can magnify your reach of generosity and has the ability to break through any geographic and demographic constraints.

From random acts of kindness to timely investments that take lengths of time, the generosity that educators possess is a way that through one life, the narratives of many generations of lives can be positively changed. There is a ripple effect that can take place. Robert Kennedy said, "Each time a man stands up for an ideal, or acts to improve the lot of others, or strikes out against injustice, he sends out a tiny ripple of hope, and crossing each other from a million centers of energy and daring those ripples build a current which can sweep down the mightiest walls of oppression and resistance." I venture to say that this tiny ripple of hope can come through the act of generosity.

Education itself does not stand in isolation of the people who form that education in children's lives. As education continues to be the great equalizer, the generous acts of educators are the vehicles through which this equality can exist. Know that the work you do is important. Know that the work you do is life changing and know that the work you do does matter. Continue to do this work generously and it is through this culture of generosity I believe we can not only make positive change but also make positive change with perpetuate itself.

Receiving Generosity

The disclaimer to being generous is that to give something, you need to have something to give. Although monetary philanthropy is one way to show generosity, there still needs to be an expendable amount of something; time, talent or resources, to give. Do not allow your generosity bank to go down to zero, or worst yet, to reach a deficit. We have all reached the point where we have felt that we have had nothing left to give. Not taking the time to replenish your generosity reserves can lead to burn out or resentment. It's important to know when we not only need to replenish our own system, but when we need to ask for and receive generosity ourselves. We need to keep amazing educators going strong and equip them with the energy that they need to meet the demands that face them everyday.

Taking the time to refuel and replenish your generosity supply is crucial to continuing to have something to give. Being self-aware of what recharges your generosity battery and giving yourself permission and time to be able to do so is crucial. As an introvert, taking the time throughout the day to be alone and process information allows for micro moments to recharge. I have learned the hard way that constantly being around takers and generously giving until spent can lead to a situation where recovery to where generously giving was enjoyable again took way longer than necessary. Learning from that experience, I now have go-to strategies to ensure that I don't find myself in that situation again. In addition to quick micro moments to recharge, allowing for extended moments to hit the reset button has also proven invaluable.

A lot has to do with my mental health and frame of mind. People often ask where I go on vacation since I live in Hawaii. Although it would be great to be able to reboot here where many people come to vacation, getting away off the island allows for a physical separation from the responsibilities of home and allows an opportunity to see things from a different perspective that allows me to completely recharge. This reflective time enables me to be able to get out any "bugs" in my thinking or in my way of doing things that may be lurking and hindering progress or growth. With young school aged children at home, we typically trade "paradise" for the "Happiest Place on Earth". Knowing when a complete recharge and reboot is necessary allows for the energy needed to move forward.

Another key to receiving generosity is to stay connected with others who can help to recharge your generosity energy level.

In education we say it is not good to be on an island. I live in a place that is beautiful, but isolated in the middle of the Pacific Ocean. Through leveraging technology, staying close to those who can positively uplift you when your reserves are running low is easier than ever. It is common for educational leaders or emerging leaders to feel isolated as there may be no one else within their daily circles who share the same experiences. To truly become a generous leader, getting beyond a daily survival mode is important for the growth of not only your school, but also yourself. Being a connected educator is not only profession-ally important, but also creates a space where generosity can be shared and received.

Generosity is Good for Everyone

It turns out that being generous is not only good for everyone else, but there are also researched backed health benefits to being generous. Being generous to improve our health really would be missing the point, although the added bonus doesn't hurt either. According to the *Huffington Post* article, "7 Science-Backed Reasons Why Generosity Is Good For Your Health" (www. huffingtonpost.com/2013/12/01/generosity-health_n_4323727. html) being stingy led to higher levels of the stress-hormone cortisol, being generous led to greater group success in the long run, being generous decreases the risk of early mortality increasing length of life, and psychologically improves the desire to want to be generous again. Studies also found that generos-ity was a key factor for those in happy marriages. Generosity through volunteering improves well-being and life satisfaction and decreases depression. There is scientific research to back up what we suspected all along: doing good things for others feels good because it is good for us.

In a study at the University of Zurich in Switzerland, just the thought of being generous led to increased brain activity in the regions of the brain associated with altruism and happi-ness. The study participants who were in the group required to spend money on others instead of themselves reported a higher level of happiness at the end of the experiment. Being generous created notable changes in brain activity and demonstrated that even thinking about being generous tended to make people happier (http://time.com/4857777/generosity-happiness-brain/). In addition to the obvious benefits that generosity has for the recipient, multiple research studies show that generosity also has positive benefits for the giver.

Think back to that time again when you were the recipient of someone's generosity. Did someone offer something that you desperately needed at that time? Was it just the right words at the right time? Was it a specific offer of help just when you needed it the most? Was it advice, or an opportunity, or a boost that completely transformed your life? The beauty of practicing empathy through generosity is that it does not only offer help, but more importantly, it offers hope. Now think of the times that you have offered hope through generosity to others. Being generous felt great, didn't it? Here are some simples things we can do every day to be generous towards others. Try to do one each day.

- Praise a person's strengths
- Notice a person's successes
- Encourage someone's efforts
- Believe in others
- Tell a person you appreciate them
- Eat lunch with someone
- Smile
- Offer to help someone
- Listen to someone
- Post kinds words on their door or locker
- Tell someone you like their shoes
- Smile
- Notice when a person has a new hairdo
- Send an e-card
- Tell a funny joke
- Ask someone's opinion
- Celebrate even the smallest accomplishments
- Give a public compliment
- Smile

The power of generosity is not only transformative for the person on the receiving end, but also for the generous giver as well. We know that happier people perform better and that stress stifles creativity. It is important that everyone in a school is encouraging; it doesn't always have to come top down. In fact it seems to be more effective when it comes from colleagues or non supervisors.

Generosity in Action

Puna Lava Devastation

It became international news when lava destroyed over 700 homes in the lower Puna subdivision on the Big Island of Hawaii. Thousands of residents were displaced. In addition to the families who lost their homes when the lava overtook their homes, there were additional residents who were cut off from accessing their homes as the lava destroyed roads and spewed toxic gases into the air that made any remaining areas inhabitable. The lava flow wiped out entire subdivisions and with it the homes and memories for many residents. As with any subdivision or residential area, there are children who go to the local schools and teachers who live in the area. In addition to losing their homes and possessions, these children lost access to their schools and for many, a stabilizing safe environment. The teachers who lost their homes in the areas also lost their places of employment as they not only had no place to go home to, but also no place to work. They were left homeless and unemployed by this unpredictable natural disaster that has so far lasted for months and possibly could go on for years. As the nation was gripped by the stories of devastation from the lava flow and all that it destroyed in its path, teachers from across the nation have rallied together to help dozens of fellow teachers who lost their homes, generously raising over $100,000 in just a few weeks for those whom they never met. The week that we sat down to write this book a school in the Puna area, Kua O Ka La Charter School, received the word from those doing aerial flyovers that lava closed in and overran their campus. The school was located on a historically sacred archaeological site with lowland rainforests and fishponds. Efforts are already underway to help support the students and teachers one the new school year.

Hurricane Harvey in Houston and Hurricane Irma in Florida

The 2017 Atlantic hurricane season was among one of the worst in recorded history. In addition, the devastation caused by the hurricanes in 2017 resulted in the most expensive hurricane season in the United States to date. Among the major hurricanes causing the most destruction that year: Hurricane Harvey in southern Texas, Hurricane Irma in Florida and Hurricane Maria in Puerto Rico. In total, there was over $270 billion in damages from the 17 named storms during that season which included 6 major hurricanes (Category 3, 4 and 5). According to NOAA, these hurricanes claimed the lives of over 251 people (www.ncdc. noaa.gov/billions/events/US/1980-2018).

Beyond the capabilities and scope of a federal national response, how does each town affected come back from this level of despair? From amongst the devastation arose many heroes generously giving of their time, strength, talents and funds to slowly come back from the massive catastrophe. On a large scale, the flooding in Houston in 2017 showed how natural disasters can cause widespread destruction. Entire school districts were closed down for months. Students and schools from across the nation heeded the call to band together to help. Even in the wake of their own trials and struggles, Houston educators and students rose up to do what they could to help their city come back from disaster. Grass-roots efforts, GoFundMe pages, donations, volunteer centers, student-led school organized fundraisers, many came together to do what they could to offer help and hope.

According to Teach For America's One Day Magazine "Teachers set up Amazon wish lists and GoFundMe pages to re-supply their classrooms. They unloaded truckloads of donated supplies that arrived in convoys from around the nation. One example: Prince George's County Public Schools in Maryland sent backpacks and set a goal of raising $132,000 (a dollar for every student in the county) for Houston schools. Within days of the first cloud break, district and network schools in Houston pulled off the massive logistical task of amassing volunteers to clean, refurnish and re-stock schools and find their students wherever they had scattered (www. teachforamerica.org/one-day-magazine/after-floods-receded-houston-educators-and-students-rose).

Needs are present everywhere and at all times and examples of people's generous acts are everywhere. The beauty of generosity is that it could be small, it could be large, and it could be a whole bunch of small coming together to be something large. Perpetuating the culture of generosity can make a difference in the lives of many.

Life-Changing Opportunities

I didn't know what to expect when I got a call from the governor's office. "Can you be down here in an hour?", the secretary asked. "Oh yeah sure," I responded while looking down at the t-shirt, shorts and rubber slippers (flip-flops) I was wearing. Guess there was no going to summer school class, because today would be life altering.

As an educator there are many opportunities each day that we give to others. Whether large or small we have the power to do so in our schools and classrooms. Remember, education is the great equalizer so it is especially important as Americans to be generous with these opportunities to our school populations that have been underrepresented, underserved and most vulnerable regardless if they are children or adults.

When I was 20 years old I was given the opportunity of a lifetime. The chairwoman of the Hawaii State Board of Education called to let me know that there was a vacant position they needed to fill and wanted to submit my name for consideration. I had previously been a student representative to the board my senior year of high school and had worked alongside many of the top educational leaders, supporting their reform efforts in Hawaii. It was my dream to continue those making a difference in schools. Yet it seemed like an impossible long shot for someone who had no family connections and just a couple college credits under his name. Then the call came in as I was preparing to duck into a summer school class. The governor wants to meet in an hour. I hightailed it home to grab one of my few nice aloha shirts and headed to the capitol building.

I sat down with the governor and he asked a few questions that to this day I'm not sure if I answered correctly. He cut to the chase and just asked, "all I want to know is if you can make the tough decisions." I quickly said that I could because my votes will be based upon the advice of educators along with feedback from parents and students. He said, "When I was your age I could probably do the same, wait right here." He quickly talked to his communication officer to issue a press release and media statement and I was sworn in a few days later.

I tell the story because of the generosity of opportunity that those who had influence and power gave freely. What I found out later was that there were many people who had urged the governor, including his wife, to give the kid a shot. The governor could have appointed a well-known experienced individual as some of the ripping letters to the editors exclaimed. And yet he gave me an opportunity to contribute to public education in Hawaii and expend his own political capital to do so. Now as a seasoned administrator of 25 years I hope that I have fulfilled that trust. Giving opportunity to those who don't have the same privileges as other is a generous gift, one that I try to continue to pass on when the opening presents itself.

Here are just a few ways we can be generous with opportunities to build culture, relationships and capacity in our schools.

◆ Give opportunities for students and adults to develop their own voice. Rather than forcing our own opinions on them we need to give them time and space to creatively express their own thoughts and ideas. This can mean supporting and promoting opportunities for rich discussions on and off line, blogging or podcasting, or public speaking forums. We can help by offering engaging questions that help them to think deeply. Allow for disagreements with you, hearing their ideas, so participants can walk away comfortable that they can have open conversations. After all good people can agree to disagree. Once they are able to connect their thoughts to their voice you have helped them to activate a powerful instrument that is empowering.

◆ Give a seat at the table to allow for meaningful decision-making for those who have not traditionally been involved in taking responsibility for school improvement. Just as I had jurisdiction over statewide school policy and a $1.8 billion budget at a young age I fully believe that students and teachers need to be a part of building and strengthening a school. Administrators you are key to this you can unlock a dynamo of creative energy that can not only boost morale and ownership it helps you to connect the key stakeholders to the work of achieving your shared goals. Authentic empowerment of teachers and students fosters ownership of success, improves school culture, and builds trust in the team. It increases their value, motivates and gives a purpose for their learning. Empowerment ultimately builds sustaining leadership capacity at a school and strengthens the power of the collective.

◆ Allow for people to take risks without fear of punishment and reprisal. Not all things go the way we planned. That's why when we go out with a reel and rod on a boat we call it fishing not catching. Opportunities are just a chance for success not a guarantee so let's not be surprised when things don't work. Create an environment that allows others to challenge the status quo, breaking down traditions and barriers to learning. Don't penalize failure but see that as an opportunity to learn and grow together. Innovation is not something that just happens the first time. It takes many iterations to get it exactly right. It is through creating a safe culture for risk-taking that generously allows for positive connections to happen.

◆ Put yourself in other people's shoes. When a teacher has a need, reflect upon what it is like being a teacher, then make decisions that present benefit for both the school and faculty member. This process works likewise for students. It may mean going the extra mile to coach faculty members. It may mean thinking outside of the box to try to make schools exciting places for students to learn. It means not tolerating toxic educational practices that don't engage or empower others. It may mean taking the time to learn and figure out what the real problems are. These are the steps that empathetic educators take to make things happen.

◆ Share your knowledge and expertise with the world. A simple tweet or Facebook post can travel all around the world in milliseconds. Whether an inspiring quote, new educational idea, research on brain development, or an exciting activity at school, the ability for educators to share information with people around the world is something that has never been possible before. The ability to tell a story about their profession and their learning may be something that influences or encourages other school leaders. Online connections through professional learning networks span time and space, offering wonderful opportunities for people to build relationships. Having the opportunity to converse over social media with other educators educational leaders provides a sense of comfort and ability to commiserate, and to look each other in the eye virtually and say to each other, "I understand; I've been there and done that." It is something that may allow you and others to take more risks because people say, "you have a good idea," or, "we tried that but we had to do this to make it work." These relationships sustain you so you can continue to be your best.

Wishful thinking perhaps, but changing the culture of generosity needs to begin somewhere. Generosity should not be forced upon others but can be a powerful tool to connect, build relationships and invest in others. It can change the culture of your school. I am sure you have many greats ideas on what you can do. Think about other ways you can be generous with giving opportunities to those at your school. Share them out on social media with the tag #EdWriteNow.

9

Connecting with the Center

Bringing Passion into the Schoolhouse

Sean Gaillard

Connecting with Gershwin

George Gershwin almost got me tossed out of Reynolds Auditorium.

Perhaps, I would have been the first eleven-year-old to be thrown out of this historic site for actually enjoying the music of the classic American composer. It may be rare for a 5th grader such as myself to stand as a fan of classical music, but I was quickly becoming a fan. During those days, I had a propensity for profanity, mastered the art of flipping off my Math Teacher behind her back in the most subtle of ways and on occasion I would engage in hand-to-hand combat in the bathroom during recess.

Now, I found a new kind of trouble to get into as I was standing on the auditorium chair attempting to conduct the Winston-Salem Symphony Orchestra as they performed Gershwin's "Rhapsody in Blue." The soaring harmonies of Gershwin's "Rhapsody in Blue" were searing into my soul and the music compelled me to get on my feet and join that orchestra.

Students were laughing and few heads turned with a thick layer of incredulity. I did not care. It was a typical episode for me to engage in silly antics that drew negative attention. I was a frequent flyer in such scenes as silent lunch, no recess, check-marked name on the board on some permutation of all three of those combined.

Hearing Gershwin's "Rhapsody" opened a new door for me. These were new sounds that were inviting me into a new world filled with harmony, creativity and promise. I could see the contagious excitement on the faces of the musicians on stage. The conductor was wildly moving in a way that reminded me of dancing. I wanted in to that world. I wanted to be a part of that joy. In fact, I had never felt such a feeling of belonging from a group of grown-ups and yet I was a stranger in the crowd of elementary school students.

We had previously attended a series of field trips that were meant to stir musical appreciation in the youth of my community. Our local orchestra sponsored these trips where we were exposed to a different section of musicians. One month it was the brass section. The next were the woodwinds and so on. My little cadre of friends showed great disdain for these trips. Classical Music was deemed as being uncool and did not reach any kind of credibility as the musical stylings of Van Halen, Rush and AC/DC did.

I went along with the group disapproval for these trips as I was desperately seeking connection and acceptance. Being a new student to this school, I craved belonging. Adding to my detachment is the fact that I was the only person of color in my class. I was a stranger in North Carolina coming from the faraway land of California. My music of choice was The Beatles and I had suffered much ridicule for being an alien from the West Coast listening to "old music." I wanted to be accepted by this group. I wanted to be picked first for kickball. I wanted to feel the embrace of any kind of connection.

Joining in the ridicule of the gaseous noises of the brass instruments or mocking the various hairstyles of the string section, a small part of my heart ached. I loved these field trips in secret. The musician presenters were translating for me a language I always heard but could not understand or explain. These were mystical experiences for me hearing how instruments worked and played together. My need for acceptance with the guys outweighed the wonder of Music.

Perhaps, the pretense of going along with the crowd moved me to escape during that performance of "Rhapsody in Blue." Maybe my subconscious was tired of the charade and the wild, raucous melodies of Gershwin ignited me to stand on my feet. I was carried away in that moment and my 10-year-old self was blissfully embracing the musical power of the moment.

My fabled conducting career arrived at an abrupt end as my 5th Grade Teacher, Mrs. McMonagle, guided me back into my seat. It was a firm hand and I thought I was headed for another round of doom in silent lunch.

What happened next was another dot she connected for me in my journey.

It was a nod.

This nod roughly translated to me: "Go ahead and conduct, but please stay seated."

My hands slowly went up and I finished my conducting of the Gershwin's masterpiece. There was much ridicule that followed after that particular field trip. I was hurt by the words, admonishments and exclusion. I was determined to find that majestic song that stirred something in me. I remember rushing home and discovering that my mother had a copy of the record. Repeated listenings of "Rhapsody in Blue" followed and I now had another dot to connect towards my journey in the love for Music.

Connecting to Passion

Looking back, I often wonder what would have happened if Mrs. McMonagle had not encouraged me during that performance. That encouragement led me down a path to pursue a love of the Arts. The reassurance freed me from my silo and energized me to have a lifelong and unabashed love for all things Music. What if I did not receive that gentle permission from my teacher to quietly express my passion? Would I have the same love for Music? What if I was punished for causing a disturbance during that permission? Would the passion I have for Music germinated in some other way?

A simple nod connected me to a passion that has reaped so many benefits in so many ways.

Passion is the ignition that has fueled many great things for artists, innovators and creators. Beethoven's 9th Symphony would not have happened if the composer did have the passion for making a grand musical statement. Michelangelo's paintings across the ceiling of the Sistine Chapel would not attract thousands of visitors every year if it were not for his passion for visual expression. Billie Holliday's musical and political statement expressed in "Fruit Tree" would not resonate today if it were not for her passion in singing the blues in a profound way reflecting a sense of social justice.

This passion connects to building relationships. A teacher who is passionate about their respective content area resonates in a profound way for students. Think about one of your teachers who walked into your classroom unabashedly excited to share a new concept on the Periodic Table of Elements. This person may have been so passionate about the Periodic Table of Elements that they encouraged the class to dress up as their favorite element for Halloween.

Actually, this happened to me in college during Chemistry Class. Imagine the teacher's passion igniting non-Science major college students in desperate need of credits to dress up willingly as their favorite element without dangling a grade or the promise of extra credit. It happened. This teacher's contagious passion for Science and the Halloween Element Dress-Up reached our local television news affiliate.

Passion is the denominator for so many ways to compel positive change and sustaining relationships. Classrooms and schoolhouses are transformed when this passion is in the foreground of the vision and mission.

We must also remember that passion is a two-way street in the schoolhouse. Students *and* teachers must be able to feel free to share their respective passions for learning, interests, pursuits and hobbies. In other words, we typically align this with students expressing their passion. There are many vehicles for students do this in creative projects that run the gamut from Makerspace, Project-Based Learning, Passion Projects, Google 10% Time. Teachers are often looked to be the sage on the stage or the facilitator compelling students to share and express their passions and gifts. The paradigm has to shift to a norm where teachers can take risks and share their passions, too. When I was a classroom teacher, everyone knew I loved music and films. The classroom walls were filled with posters of The Beatles, John Coltrane and The Who. I encouraged students to share their music posters as well. Any time I could talk Music with students was an opportunity to build a relationship. Incidentally, it's important for school leaders to follow suit. Modeling our passion about a hobby or some aspect of educational practice, school leaders can help ignite a culture of positivity and creativity fueled by sincere passion.

Sharing our passions unabashedly in the classroom or schoolhouse is meant to build that community of possibility for our students. Placing more passion in the day-to-day operations of the schoolhouse will only uplift students. Students need any opportunity given to express their gifts, ideas and passions. It is part of our calling as educators to make that happen.

As educators, we have a responsibility to model the passion we wish for our students and colleagues to exhibit for the work we share. Students will make the classic complaint that the class is boring. A teacher may respond that their role is not to entertain but to teach. A teacher may voice dread in attending yet another dry faculty meeting due to the principal's ponderous agenda. A school leader may respond that it is the responsibility of the teacher to act in a professional, adult manner and engage in meeting discussion. Teachers and Administrators may express the lack of time to plan an activity filled with passion. How many of these excuses have you heard?

♦ I don't have time to plan that.
♦ I have to feel really passionate to come across that way.
♦ I tried to dress up as a historical figure and they laughed at me.
♦ My district does not have the funds for an activity like that.

- ◆ I am not that type of educator who entertains like that. I am not an actor.
- ◆ Only those (insert category or adjective here) type of teachers do that and they are all weird.
- ◆ Only those (insert category or adjective here) type of principals do that and they are all weird.
- ◆ I am not a leader.
- ◆ I am shy.
- ◆ I didn't get into teaching to juggle or perform. They are supposed to do the work!
- ◆ I didn't become a principal to make friends. I have test scores to raise!
- ◆ Doing that does not align with the pacing calendar! I have to get this unit done before benchmark testing next week! Maybe some other time?
- ◆ Since when did being passionate help someone get a job?

We can come up with many excuses not to express passion in the schoolhouse. Excuses do not serve the noble work we do for students. We impede the catalyst for great change by excusing passion from the actions we do to serve and support children. When it does come to sharing our passion as educators in the schoolhouse, we cannot permit power to excuses.

Here are some quick solution-based responses to encountering excuses from colleagues:

- ◆ Connect with your Professional Learning Network (PLN). There are many groups who can give you real-time suggestions and support to empower you to rise above the excuses. Follow hashtags like #JoyfulLeaders, #PrincipalsInAction, #MomsAsPrincipals, #DadsAsPrincipals, #EduGladiators for support. Some of these groups also exist as Voxer Groups.
- ◆ Attend an EdCamp. Many growth-minded educators frequent these educational "un"-conferences. Participating in these free events can help build your PLN and/or connect with thought partners in real time for support.

♦ Engage in the purpose of the excuse. Sometimes a simple question as, "Why would that thinking best help our kids?" in response to an excuse can diffuse the negativity.

♦ Invite the individual who provides the excuse to collaborate with you. It might be that the excuse from a naysayer is their own way of crying for help or wishing to be invited to collaborate.

Passion for the work we do in the classroom as a teacher or in the wheelhouse as a school leader is a must. It cannot be a canned performance or a bumper sticker slogan. It has to come from the heart in a relentless and sincere way that is inspiring students to reach greater heights to change the world. It is even better when that passion is encouraged and supported with a vibrant, shared vision held by all in the schoolhouse.

Connecting to the Practice

There are many ways to bring passion to the conversation in the schoolhouse. Taking practical and intentional steps will provide support in transforming a school culture. The key is not to relegate it to a one-time event. It has to be a collaborative and proactive enterprise involving students, teachers, staff members and families. The more voices unified in the sharing of passions, the better the chances are at building sustainability for the culture of the school in a positive way.

Here are some suggested next steps to connecting to passion:

♦ Embed a Passion Moment in the classroom. Have students share how a particular lesson, activity or concept connects to their passions.

♦ Create a Passion Wall where students have artifacts and examples of things that inspire them or reflect their passions. A similar wall could be displayed by the faculty in the lounge or common area of a schoolhouse.

♦ Devote an entire Faculty Meeting where teachers and staff share their passions.

♦ Encourage teachers to embed one lesson in a unit where the content is devoted to why the teacher loves the content of the area they teach. A math teacher can share their love for theroems or an art teacher could transform their classroom into a gallery devoted to their favorite artist. Perhaps, a science teacher could even share their favorite musician? It does not necessarily have to be devoted to one's assigned content area to teach.

Connecting to the Why

A word that is tossed around in educational circles either with reverent, hushed tones or misguided ignorance is relationships. We use the word as a signpost to make a profound point in a blog post or TED Talk. It may be used with brittle disdain amongst colleagues in the parking lot or faculty lounge. Administrators may use it to voice a complaint about why a teacher is proving to be ineffective.

We speak with conviction about this concept of relationships. Most educators recognize the value of relationships. I do not believe anyone would intentionally diminish the magnitude of its importance whether they agree with its value or not.

We can all attest to some educator having a positive impact on our lives. This impact is often described as being far-reaching and life-changing. Individual educators have filled our shelves with poignant stories on that one person that made a significant difference in our lives. These stories are celebratory, insightful and moving. They appeal to the better angels of our collective nature as educators. The intentional connection we have as educators with students and colleagues creates a culture that inspires, builds trust and compels meaningful change.

As we pursue the nature of the way behind establishing authentic relationships as educators, we must consider the following questions:

Questions to consider:

- ◆ *Do we believe in the social and emotional responsibility as educators to build up, inspire and motivate all students?*

- *Why pursue the necessity to build authentic relationships in the schoolhouse?*
- *Do our actions align with a shared vision in our school serving all students?*
- *How does a visitor to our school know that we value relationships?*

Education is a human enterprise and we must believe that the work we are doing is serving a noble purpose for the children we serve. As educators we are called to inspire students to pursue dreams, change the world and add meaning to our world. Relationship building is an integral part of any teaching and learning in the schoolhouse. See Rita Pierson's TED Talk to get a visceral and unforgettable sense of the magic of relationships with teachers and students.

Realistically speaking, not all educators value relationships. Even though we have sound research and data backing the claim that relationships matter, some educators may not see the merit. There are emotional stories that display the significance of relationships on students and educators alike. Some educators may not receive these inspirational stories in the way that they are meant to move the listener.

How do we compel others to get back to the Why of Connecting? How do we start the conversation with our colleagues to not only buy-in to the concept of developing but to also engage in dynamic and inspired action?

We start by harnessing and sharing that passion by taking the first step when it comes to connecting with the Why.

Connecting to the Center

As a beginning principal, I thought I had arrived. I had the degrees and certification to prove it. My bookshelf was filled with books whose respective covers illuminated my self-proclaimed brilliance. I could drop the names of respected educators of varying levels of renown and cite a witty quote from one of their books. I subscribed to the right magazines and passed on articles in a condescending way to other teachers. Feeling emboldened with the buzz of being what I thought was an antidote to my predecessor, I believed my hype. The vigor of the moment of being a newly-appointed principal caused me to casually dismiss the wisdom of my mentors, coaches and supervisors.

I remember my assistant superintendent, someone I value and uphold as a true mentor, giving me powerful advice. Her wisdom still resonates with me and I am grateful for the lesson that was shared. When she shared with me her advice right before I started my first principalship, my misguided bravado drowned out something so essential. It took me a few months of being checked down to size and reaching out to my assistant superintendent that she reiterated the same wisdom. I had forgotten my purpose for serving others and staying focused on a vision. The mechanics of leadership were more of my focus during those earlier days in my principalship and I had forgotten the core of what drove me into our noble profession as educators in the first place. I felt distanced from the staff and students I was serving due to hanging onto the superficial title of principal. I needed to re-connect myself with the purpose that had driven me to a person for others as an educator.

Seeking the connection of this particular mentor gave me the reminder to tap into my passion an educator. It renewed a sense of purpose and enlarged my focus on truly doing what is best for all students. She gently reminded me of her past advice and encouraged me to share with the faculty as soon as possible. I wasn't admonished or belittled. It was like I was getting that gentle nod of reassurance from Mrs. McMonagle all over again. With a new appreciation for deep listening and the wisdom of my mentor, I followed a simple strategy to begin an initial conversation with our teaching staff. This strategy re-fueled our purpose as a faculty team and helped us to define our why in serving and supporting our kids.

At the next faculty meeting, I walked with in a humble heart prepared to share, connect and support. Carrying a large pad of newsprint and a magic marker, I demonstrated the following steps.

The Center Strategy

1. Write down the name of school in the center of the paper.
2. Elicit ideas from the staff on the things that happen in the school. It may involve the following examples: teaching, grading, homework, projects, discipline procedures, etc.
3. Ask for ideas on which of the examples ring as the most important. There will be varying responses and that is all right with the flow of discussion. The aim is to generate a conversation.
4. After you have facilitated conversation and sharing, simply write the word, "STUDENTS," in the center of the paper.
5. Share that our students are our purpose in the schoolhouse.
6. Share examples for how and why that is happening in your schoolhouse today. Ask your colleagues to share examples as well.

Taking an intentional pause to start a conversation with colleagues can inspire momentum, change and shifts that will enhance enterprise to make great things happen in a schoolhouse. Conversations centered around serving students does impact the culture.

Embedding a "We" Approach models the connections we wish to foster with our students. Placing students at the center serves as powerful reminder that must echo for all individuals collaborating in service and support of our students. It also provides a sense of unity for all members of the school staff. Unifying the staff cannot just be relegated to one faculty meeting or a retreat activity. Educators must commit to reminding each other of the purpose in a schoolhouse. It must involve students at the center and it must be echoed relentlessly. Placing students at the center of all intentional actions and decisions builds a sustainable positive culture. Furthermore, it enhances the bond to reinforce authentic relationships for all.

Bringing the Passion

Visiting classrooms one day at Lexington Middle School, where I am honored to serve and support as principal, I noticed a life-size poster of Spider Man displayed in one of our 7th Grade ELA Classrooms. Being an unabashed fan of this particular super-hero from my youth, I asked the teacher there where he found such a cool-looking poster. The teacher was enthused to share and we began an expansive and very geeky conversation on comic books, superheroes, myths. We were not talking shop and the line between supervisor and employee had dissipated. Our conversation would not look out of place at a local comic book store where friends were chatting away their various passions on the nature of superheroes. We began to quiz each other and cite different elements of favorite film adaptations and graphic novels. A real kinship was forming and I believe we both realized we had an entry point to further connections as colleagues and teammates.

I suggested to the teacher that he should display more super-hero ephemera in his classroom. I shared that it would be a great entry point for discussion in building relationships with his students. I reminded him that comic books and graphic novels are a form of literacy and could align with the curriculum in such a cool, creative way. Briefly, I gave him an example of my classroom decor during my high school English teaching days. I shared with him how I had album covers and posters covering the walls displaying my love for Music. I detailed how that display fueled much debate, discovery and discussion on Music between my students and myself.

I felt myself giving this young, beginning teacher a nod. He returned the nod back and I noticed his classroom was filled with comic books, superhero posters and graphic novels a few days later.

Imagine a school where passions are shared relentlessly. You have that nod now. What does that look like? Your turn.

10

Connecting with Dreams to Create a World Class Culture

Danny Bauer

A lot of school leaders I know say they have the best job in the world.

They don't.

I do.

I have the privilege of working with the most inspiring leaders from around the world. We gather weekly and meet online to discuss two topics that light me up inside: leadership and education. We gather in order to find clarity within our high stakes leadership positions while solving the greatest challenges we face on our campuses. The questions and challenges we discuss vary each week, but foundationally, we are often asking a similar question as we keep digging.

Maybe the question starts out, "How do I motivate my staff to do more to for kids?"

Soon it evolves into, "How are you building relationships with your staff?" Because relationships matter people!

I am not a *kids first* school leader. I am a *people first* school leader because the underlying assumption is that if my staff feels known, appreciated, and respected they'll do great work for kids. And that's true.

Then there's the idea that Dan Pink is famous for: that autonomy, mastery, and purpose is how you build a world class organization (and thus do more for kids).

But what I'm fired up about right now is the untapped potential that schools could massively leverage to build a good to great culture.

What I'm talking about are dreams. Yes, dreams.

The secret I want to share with you today is that as a leader, if you tap into, understand, and find a way (believe me, it is possible) to make your people's dreams a reality, then anything is possible!

More on that in just a second . . .

But first a story about a 90 day plan and being a new principal.

Getting to Know My Staff As a New Principal

It doesn't matter if you are a principal or not, any educator can use these principles found within this chapter as they are universal. The only thing that will change is context and maybe some of the approach. However, I guarantee the results will still be incredible and lead to creating anything from a world class classroom, grade level, department, campus, or even district.

As a new principal, it was truly important for me to know (and really know) who I was working with. Obviously that comes with time, but I think you can fast track relationship building when done with intentionality.

My major takeaway from the text, *The First 90 Days*, by Michael Watkins was to be focused on results that I wanted to achieve:

- ◆ At the end of the first day
- ◆ At the end of the first week
- ◆ At the end of the first month
- ◆ At the end of the first quarter (90 days)

I had a variety of goals that mattered and by the end of the 2nd month of entering my new campus I wanted to have accomplished meeting with every staff member for a 15 minute informal interview.

Don't worry . . . I wasn't evaluating who I was going to keep on campus or who I wanted to let go. My goal was quite simple: I wanted to know the other human beings that I was going to be spending a lot of time with. I wanted to know the people that would be executing the vision I had for the school.

There is a quote that I love regarding vision that I think every leader needs to memorize:

"Write the vision down so that those who read it will RUN!"

There is such great wisdom found in this phrase. One, I think it's important to note that inspiring visions inspire those to run toward it. Two, when the vision is inspiring the people execute it.

Leaders come up with the vision, but their people implement it.

Lao Tzu agrees, "A leader is best when people barely know he exists, when his work is done, his aim fulfilled, they will say: we did it ourselves."

Now you might be thinking, "Wait, wait, wait Danny . . . what does all this talk about vision have to do with dreams . . . and isn't this book about education?"

It's all connected.

A leader inspires her people to execute the vision and the magic truly happens when the people within the organization (that could be a school staff, but also students of a classroom) actually believe that it was their idea and that they did it themselves. That is the power of ownership and a truly captivating vision.

And the best way to get people inspired . . .

The best way to get people to own the dream and "do the work" . . .

Is to understand their dreams and make it a reality.

So with this understanding, I embarked on a challenging goal. To sit with just over 100 staff members and get to know them better as people in 15 minutes.

Here is how I did it.

Getting Practical: 15 Minute Meet and Greets

School leaders today need to double down on the investment of understanding and getting to know their people at a deep level. I am more convinced of this than ever. When I first accepted a position as principal at the last school I led it was of extreme importance to really understand who my people were so I set an audacious goal of meeting with every staff member for 15 minutes of undivided attention and great conversation.

The steps were actually quite simple:

1. Send everyone a link to my calendar so they could pick a time that works best for them
2. Staff then filled out a short survey (you can get the questions here: betterleadersbetterschools.com/15minutequestions)
3. Meet and talk about their lives and interests (not school!)

There is a method to my madness.

In Step One I used a tool called Calendly. There are free and paid versions; the free version is more than appropriate for scheduling this kind of meeting. Calendly is a perfect tool because it integrates with your calendar and you can set up meeting boundaries (days and times you are available) before sending out to staff. Then your people have the ability to pick the perfect time that works for them given the boundaries you already set up. I really like this approach because it eliminates the biggest waste of time ever (back and forth scheduling meetings via email – yuck!) and *honors* the precious time of your staff and gives them multiple options to set up a meeting.

In Step Two I sent out a short survey via Google Forms. The questions I asked are as follows:

1. What do you want to know about your new principal?
2. What do you want me to know about you?
3. What is your favorite snack or treat?
4. Who are your favorite music artists?
5. When is your birthday?
6. Share 3 traditions at [NAME OF YOUR SCHOOL].

7. Share 3 strengths of [NAME OF YOUR SCHOOL].
8. Share 3 opportunities for growth.
9. What challenges do we face as an organization?
10. Who has been instrumental in shaping the organization?
11. If you were me, what would you focus your attention on this year?

Here is a link to the questions I asked my people, feel free to steal them here: https://betterleadersbetterschools.com/15minutequestions. Here you will notice a variety of questions. Some speak to the traditions, challenges, and history of the school. Other questions focus on some surface level relationship building. Some questions I used clandestinely and would randomly show up at classrooms with favorite treats or play individual's favorite song at staff meetings (and have a fun vote on whose song is this with a gift card given to the person who correctly guessed first).

By Step Three I would have read through each response and potentially written some follow up questions to dig deeper. However, the main focus of the 15 minute meet and greet was to actively listen and learn as much about my people as possible. It was a challenge to focus only on learning about my people and avoid as much school talk as possible. This was also a challenge for my staff, but in the long run it paid off. You can write your notes on a computer, but I preferred to use a notebook and pencil.

Here are some example questions that I asked (which are also available at https://betterleadersbetterschools.com/15minutequestions):

1. Tell me about your family.

    a. Are you married?
    b. When is your anniversary?
    c. How did you meet?
    d. What does your partner do?

2. Do you have kids?

    a. What are their names? Birthdays?
    b. What do you love most about your kids?

3. What are your hobbies? What recharges your battery outside of school?
4. What is your "Why"? Why do you do what you do?
5. What's the last book or movie you really enjoyed?
6. If I gave you $100 right now, how would you spend it?
7. If you weren't a teacher, what would you do for a profession?
8. Anything else you'd like me to know about you?
9. What questions do you have for me?

Surprisingly, the asking wasn't difficult for them, the answering about family and hobbies was very difficult for some of my staff. Clearly, they weren't used to (nor maybe interested in) connecting on a deeper level as opposed to clocking in and out of their J-O-B, but in my experience, world class organizations are integrated. They aren't clear separations between home and work. Not only do they call themselves "family," but they act like it too. Given the discomfort of some staff, I recommend pushing through. If you ever are going to build a world class culture, it's important to live out your principles. Strong core values act like a magnet. They attract the type of talent you want as a leader and repel those that would be more successful somewhere else. Please note that the last two questions are really important. "Anything else" is a great open-ended and broad question that elicits information that will almost always surprise and delight you. And it's always important to leave time to allow your people to learn more about you too (and no question should be off limits in my opinion).

If I were to do this activity again, I would suggest a few things to keep in mind:

◆ Leave buffers between meetings in case they go long or in case you need a break.
◆ Spread out meetings over multiple days. I "batched" the meetings so I engaged in multiple back-to-back meetings over the course of hours in a day. This left me absolutely drained!
◆ Use the questions above as a template and not a formula that all questions must be asked or followed in a certain

order. It's most important to ask what you are interested in learning (this will come through). The secret is in the follow up questions that are part improvisation and part active listening. By always digging just a bit deeper, you find out pure gold in terms of your people's histories and motivations.

◆ If you're like me, you want to capture and document the process. I did this by taking a selfie and writing one fun fact I learned and shared on Twitter. This almost backfired on me. Although my heart was to promote and celebrate my people, some were very self conscious and didn't want their picture online. Some people wanted to know ahead of time so they could have done makeup or wore a different outfit. This was a surprise to me, but a great learning lesson, so tell people ahead of time if you want to do a selfie and social media post and ask for permission. Let your people know it's okay to decline this as well.

This activity paid huge dividends for me and absolutely accelerated the building of relationships. I was able to call on this treasure trove of information, I could use to build stronger relationships and inspire my people to a higher level within our most important work in education. My final tip is to meet with everyone. Don't miss one person! I was shocked to find out that I was the first principal at my last campus to meet with office staff, lunch staff, and custodians. This made me quite proud to and again speaking of ROI, there was nothing that the office, lunch staff, or custodians wouldn't do for me because I took out a little bit of my precious time to get to know them as human beings.

Although this activity served me well, the next activities I am about to share are like jet fuel for creating a world class organization. I wish I had known them when I was at my last campus, but I'm so excited that they are in my toolbelt today and that I can share them with you. By understanding your people's deepest desires and longings of their hearts, you can absolutely inspire them to do much more than anyone thought was possible within your organization. It is absolutely the secret sauce of many top organizations. Let's start next with a simple idea everyone has heard of, but no one uses within organizations – the bucket list.

What Do You Want To Accomplish Before You Die?

The following activities I learned from my new hero, Cameron Herold. He is known as the "CEO Whisperer" and is a top-tier executive coach. I learned about him and his work by attending the 2018 World Business Executive Coaching Summit in order to keep my skill set sharp and provide excellent coaching to my school leader clients I serve. The following activities (bucket list, dream 101, and can you imagine wall) were either mentioned in his WBECS session, "Creating a World Class Culture" or can be found in his book called, *Double Double*.

As educators we often "Start with the end in mind." We should do this not only in planning rigorous units of study, but with planning our lives with intentionality as well. Bucket lists are great tools to use and get people to consider what they really want to do that's memorable with the precious time they have on this planet.

> **Why, you do not even know what will happen tomorrow. What is your life? You are a mist that appears for a little while and then vanishes.**
>
> **(James 4:14)**

I love the quote above because it captures the impermanence of life. By describing life as a mist that appears and then vanishes quickly, we see that our time here is precious – we must not waste it!

While I was dating my wife, she introduced me to a fascinating show called, *No Tomorrow*. The premise is quite simple. There was a very conservative and risk averse character (Evie) who falls for a handsome and daring man, Xavier, who crosses off one bucket list item each day he is alive. To say his life is exciting is an understatement. The problem with Xavier is that he thinks the world is about to end in the very near future, so he has a very real motivation to live fully – right now! Obviously, this is a ridiculous premise for our lives, but the essence of the show is true. It is exciting to truly live right now and create memories that will last forever while engaging in activities we've always wanted to do.

According to Cameron Herold this is an underutilized activity within most organizations, but those that investigate bucket lists with their people have a far better shot to creating a world class culture.

The premise is quite simple: have your people share their dreams via a bucket list, then help those dreams become a reality.

Zig Ziglar is famous for observing, "You will get all you want in life, if you help enough other people get what they want."

That's the secret of bucket lists. If you can make others' dreams come true, there is nothing they won't do for you and your organization. Here's how to do it.

Getting Practical: The Bucket List

This doesn't have to be rocket science. The most important aspect is to give people a heads up you will be discussing and acting on the information they share.

Here is how I did this activity within the leadership community I run at Better Leaders Better Schools:

1. Share your bucket list – model.
2. Ask people to come to the meeting with their bucket list or give them actual time during an all staff meeting to create their own (30–60 minutes).
3. Have people share in groups of 2–4 aspects of their bucket lists.
4. Have people submit their bucket lists to you.
5. Help them make their dreams come true.

Share Your Bucket List – Model
Some people might not know where to start (heck, maybe even you the reader is lost right now!). So give them an example of how to create a bucket list. Google is your friend here and by searching "bucket list examples" one will see a ridiculous amount

of resources. But there is no better way to share an example, than sharing your own bucket list. This has the added benefit of being vulnerable and sharing the special things you want to accomplish before your time on this planet is over.

Here is an example of my bucket list (https://workflowy.com/s/FFWU.ZawjcwSBH0). I used a tool called WorkFlowy that is free (signup here: https://workflowy.com/invite/36e2fe7c.lnx) because it is great for creating outlines that expand and collapse in a visually appealing manner. Even if you don't use WorkFlowy, you can draft your bucket list on your favorite word processing app or note app.

Here are the categories you can consider organizing your bucket list around (shout out to my friend Charlie Cichetti for inspiring me with his own bucket list and sharing these categories):

- ◆ Adventure (e.g. Hike the Grand Canyon)
- ◆ Travel (e.g. Visit Zimbabwe)
- ◆ Family (e.g. Build enough wealth to take care of my mother and mother-in-law)
- ◆ Business/Financial (e.g. Host a popular and life transformational conference)
- ◆ Health (e.g. Get six pack abs)
- ◆ Sports (e.g. Go to the Super Bowl)
- ◆ Home/Car (e.g. Build a Zen garden in the backyard with rocks and water)
- ◆ Misc (e.g. Start a generous scholarship for students at my alma mater or school I worked in)

Ask people to come to the meeting with their bucket list or give them actual time during an all staff meeting to create their own (30–60 minutes)

Now that people have an idea of how to create a bucket list, it's their turn. The best leaders invest in their people and create time and space for them to actually engage in the work. I highly recommend giving your people an uninterrupted block of time (30 minutes) to work together in one place to create a draft of their bucket list. If they need more time they can always revise and add to their lists later. If time cannot be found to do this together, give people plenty of notice and time ahead of a meeting to come prepared with their draft bucket list.

Have People Share in Groups of 2–4 Aspects of their Bucket Lists

Next, give another 30 minutes (minimum) for people to converse, share their bucket lists, and ask questions regarding the bucket lists. This investment of time may seem counterintuitive, but believe me, if you want to create a world class culture that stands the test of time . . . if you want to create a culture where people are incredibly connected to one another and there is great synergy . . . if you want to create the type of organization that other people read about in books and case studies . . . then invest in this amount of time by investing in your people's dreams!

One neat benefit of doing this activity is that colleagues that have known each other for years (decades even) will learn something new about a peer they have spent many years with. Conversely, if you have a younger staff or a staff that is new (maybe you're new), you will get to know people at a much deeper level quickly by sharing the intimate hopes and dreams found within a bucket list. This activity will build intimacy, relationships, and trust – the building blocks of any great organization.

Have People Submit Their Bucket Lists To You

Now that the sharing is done, a leader should collect the results. This can be done by turning in hard copy artifacts or digital copies of the bucket lists. The important thing is that the leader reviews all of her people's lists in order to better understand their dreams, desires, and longings of their hearts.

Help Them Make Their Dreams Come True

And since you now understand what your people want to accomplish, help their dreams come true! Obviously, your school or district won't be sending anyone to Stonehenge anytime soon (but maybe you will . . .) the idea is to look for dreams you can make a reality.

The Stonehenge example may seem unlikely, but maybe someone within the organization owns a timeshare in the region and is willing to give it away to a colleague to help their dream come true. This may seem highly unlikely, but you will be surprised what magic can happen once you focus on making people's dreams come true.

For Cameron Herold, one bucket list item looked like this. One of his employees had never been to San Francisco and it was on her bucket list. Well, Cameron's company had work to be done in San Francisco so guess who he sent? That's right . . . his employee whose dream was to see city in the bay. How do you think she felt toward Cameron and the company after they made that dream a reality? She would do *anything* for them and would help the organization's dreams come true. What might this example look like in a school context? We all have PD funds and it's quite common for some districts and schools to invest in their people through professional development in the way of conferences. So what if Mr. T has always wanted to go to New York and there is also an amazing conference for educators in that area. This is a no brainer and not only will you make Mr. T's dreams come true, he will most likely become one of your best team members within the organization.

One more example, I created a leadership community that has over 40 members from around the world. We get together weekly to discuss education and leadership online. During one of our meetings we shared our bucket lists. What did I find out? A number of my members want to hike the Appalachian Trail. Now financially, I am not in a position to fly 5–6 people out to the trail in order to hike it. What I can do is set a date and invite others to hike the trail with me. By casting that vision and inviting others to participate, I know we will gather a small group who will hike the Appalachian Trail and even though I didn't pay for the trip, by selecting a date and casting a vision of us hiking as a community, I know that a number of my clients will meet me there in order to cross this off their bucket list. As a result, we build a deeper friendship and be able to accomplish so much more within our leadership community.

The Dream 101 Activity

The Dream 101 activity is very similar to the bucket list activity. I also learned this from Cameron Herold where he shares the ideas in his book, *Double Double*. The key here is to understand your people at a deeper level as well as understanding the dreams they have for their lives. As a leader, it is then your job to look for where you can help your people turn their dreams into reality and thus unleash the incredible creative power found in your organization. This creativity is unleashed because of the powerful bonds and relationships you form by getting to know your people intimately and taking action on things that are important again.

Earlier I shared a quote from Zig Ziglar. I'm going to share it again because this point is so incredibly important. Zig Ziglar is famous for observing:

> You will get all you want in life, if you help enough other people get what they want.

The modern day school leader is under incredible pressure for raising student achievement scores and creating (or maintaining) a high level school in the community in which she serves. The temptation is to only look at data and discuss the nuts and bolts of school: curriculum and instruction. However, I am telling you that if you help your people get what they want in life . . . yes, the life that exists outside of the school's walls . . . then anything you want to happen within the school will be much more likely to happen. In fact, I think if you act on what I share, you just might achieve things in your community you never even thought was possible.

Getting Practical: The Dream 101

Here is how I would approach the Dream 101 in the school setting.

1. Gather the entire staff and give them 30 minutes minimum to generate as many creative answers to the Dream 101 questions as possible.
2. Allow time to share.

3. Collect the answers from your people.
4. Act! Make the dreams become a reality.

Since this activity is similar to the bucket list activity I also shared, I won't go over each step in detail here. Rather, let me highlight the importance of collecting, reading, understanding, and acting on these dreams. This is just not another feel good or team building activity. It is the leader's responsibility to engage with the content created from the Dream 101 and then act where possible to make the dreams a reality.

If you want to facilitate this activity here are the questions Cameron suggests to ask:

1. Goods you'd like to buy
2. Activities you'd like to do
3. Subjects you want to learn
4. Instruments or hobbies you want to learn (or get back to)
5. Adventures/feats you want to try for the first time
6. Personal goals you want to achieve
7. Sights you want to see
8. Places you want to go

When doing this activity with his staff, Cameron learned of one interesting dream two of his employees had: they wanted to be debt free. Like many young people, these individuals had acquired quite a bit of debt because of the exorbitant cost of a college education (as well as making frivolous purchasing decisions that we all make when we are young!). At the time of doing the Dream 101, Cameron was living debt free and had been for a while. So what did he do next? He invited his employees to meet with him regularly for dinner to discuss personal finances and allow Cameron to mentor them on how to get out of debt and to be more financially responsible. Within six months, the young people Cameron mentored had either eliminated their debt entirely or substantially. Further, they began to invest in mutual funds and building lasting wealth.

I did this activity within the mastermind I lead as well. We approached it a little differently and instead of answering all these questions in 30 minutes, we tackled one question as a discussion in 5–7 minutes. As a group we talked about activities we'd like to do or get back to and one member Mark wanted to get back into running. A year ago he completed his first half-marathon and dropped a whopping 40 pounds! Then, the demands of leading a school happened and the next thing you know, he blinked, and a year went by without a lot of running. Now Mark had referred a really amazing new member to my leadership community and because of the world class culture I'm building, I want to lead by example and model a spirit of generosity. Two days later, Mark left me a voice message, "Today when I got home from work much to my surprise there was a package on my porch with a runner's watch. That was above and beyond and I just really appreciate it. So thank you very much, I will definitely put it to good use."

That is what the Dream 101 is all about (and bucket lists too), but what if there was a way to capture the dreams of not only your staff, but your students and parents too? What if you could actually inspire other people to make those dreams a reality? And what do we do with those great ideas that may not line up 100% with our vision, but the idea is still really stinkin' cool? I'll cover that in the next section.

The "Can You Imagine?" Wall

One of my good friends, Sean Gaillard, wrote a pretty cool book called *The Pepper Effect*. Once you're done with this one I encourage you to check it out (or my book called *The Better Leaders Better Schools Roadmap*). Sean's text is all about the magic that is created when a team really gels and in terms of music, arguably the best band to ever do this was The Beatles. Of course, all good things come to end at some point and The Beatles eventually broke up. Each talented musician went their separate way and tried to express himself through individual ventures. One of the most famous songs produced from these new solo acts was John Lennon's, *Imagine*. It is a beautiful song and I believe one reason it was so popular is because it captures the listener's imagination.

The song challenges us to think of a world that is much better than the one we currently live within. Like any good leader, Lennon juxtaposes the current reality with a much more idealized future and it inspires the listener to create the world of the future because it in fact is a much better place than the current reality. In a similar way, the "Can you imagine?" wall does the same exact thing as Lennon's hit song.

But unlike the other activities I shared, it is the easiest of all strategies I share to execute. All that is needed is a wall, some markers, and an open invitation for people to be creative.

Finally, think of the wall as a suggestion box where people share inspiring ideas. If you could hear someone say, "Wouldn't it be really cool if we did 'X'?" then it belongs on the wall.

Getting Practical: Create Your "Can You Imagine?" Wall

If I were to do this within a school I would cover one wall in the entrance hallway or main office covered in whiteboard material and make markers accessible to everyone that enters the building. I would highly encourage everyone (parents, students, staff, vendors – literally everyone) to add ideas to the "Can you imagine wall?" as inspiration struck. Instruct the community to write down their dreams for the school and/or district. Additionally, maybe you add a page to your school or district website where people can also add comments and ideas for a cyber "Can you imagine?" wall space. A final note on logistics – it's up to you if you want to formally "approve" every suggestion before it is formalized and put on the wall. If you elect to go this route then having markers available wouldn't work and the system you set up would be a little more controlled.

I haven't done this activity yet, but here are some examples of comments you might see in a typical school:

- ◆ Can you imagine if all seniors were accepted by their #1 stretch school?
- ◆ Can you imagine what if there were no fights or cyber bullying in our community?
- ◆ Can you imagine if all students felt safe enough to be themselves despite how they identify sexually?

+ Can you imagine if the President came to visit our school and gave a speech to the community on the importance of education?
+ Can you imagine if no students at our school were hungry or homeless?
+ Can you imagine if local businesses partnered with the school and built a robotics lab?

Now these are fictitious examples of what might be written on your "Can you imagine?" wall so please allow me to share a few examples that really happened. As I shared earlier, this activity was inspired by Cameron Herold. At the time Cameron did this activity he was the COO of a Canadian company called 1-800-GOT-JUNK.

One idea that was particularly inspiring was to somehow get 1-800-GOT-JUNK to be featured in The Harvard Business School to do a case study on the company. Because this idea was prominently displayed on 1-800-GOT-JUNK's "Can you imagine?" wall everyone that visited the company saw the inspirational ideas. One day, a 1-800-GOT-JUNK vendor was visiting the office and mentioned to the team, "Hey, I know the guy at Harvard who approves case studies. Would you like an introduction?" The rest they say, is history.

Here is one more practical example from 1-800-GOT-JUNK. They placed a really audacious idea on their imagine wall – what if our company name was featured on Starbucks cups? When Cameron saw this he admitted in *Double Double* that he thought the idea was ludicrous. However, he was inspired by his employee's drive and passion so they left the idea on there. A few months later the company was able to celebrate a major milestone – they were to be featured on 10 *million* Starbucks cups across North America for *free*! You can't imagine the exposure this would give 1-800-GOT-JUNK. Originally, Starbucks wasn't going to feature the 1-800-GOT-JUNK company name on the cup because it generally doesn't want to market for other businesses that way. However, when the employee who took charge of making this dream a reality communicated the dream to Starbucks they reversed the decision and included the company name on the cup. So what exactly did she say to persuade the powerful Starbucks to include the 1-800-GOT-JUNK name on 10 million cups? That's easy . . . she said, "But it's on our 'Can you imagine?' wall" and sent off a picture of the wall to Starbucks.

No matter if you do any of the activities discussed here, the idea boils down to what Cameron Herold identifies as the "Conceive, believe, and achieve" mantra. This is the power of vision and the power and momentum generated from turning dreams into reality.

The Most Important Dreamer – You

At the end of the day, this work matters a lot and understanding your people and the dreams they have for themselves will absolutely be the key that unlocks creating a world class school and district. However, this only works if you are the best version of yourself too. Said a different way, it matters just as much (maybe even more) to be tuned into what lights your fire and inspires you.

A major reason I am passionate about this topic is that I'm fresh off of learning and applying these concepts within the groups I lead as well as designing a vision for my life. It took about a month, but I created a document that details exactly what I want to accomplish over the next three years – by December 31st, 2021. I welcome you to checkout this detailed map of where I am headed right here: https://betterleadersbet terschools.com/vision.

Cameron Herold calls this exercise and document a "Vivid Vision", but next I will share some practical tips on how to jump start and create your very own Vivid Vision.

Getting Practical: Building Your Vivid Vision

Some of the most important and rigorous work I have done has been to create a Vivid Vision. In reality this took an incredible time investment and I worked on it off-and-on for a month.

I would invest a heavy portion of hours to work and then would need some time away from the vision before coming back to it.

Here are a few tips in order to create your own vision:

1. **Vivid Vision Notes**
2. **Why Does Vision Matter?**

   ◆ "Write the Vision down so those that read it may RUN!" – Habakkuk 2:2
   ◆ "Where there is no vision people perish" – Proverbs 29:18
   ◆ World Class Athletes use visualization; so should world class businesses and schools
   ◆ People respond to a challenge. Vision is a target on a map. When your people know where you're going three years out; they have a better sense of how they can contribute and where they need to step up.
   ◆ Incredibly rewarding for staff to help achieve the vision.

3. **Vivid Vision**

   ◆ 3–5 page document
   ◆ Focus on where, don't worry about how
   ◆ Turn off your computer
   ◆ Get out of your normal routine. Get into nature. Ditch technology if possible. Dream big dreams.
   ◆ Think outside the box – if it is bizarre or unlikely definitely include it.
   ◆ 3 years out.
   ◆ What does your company look like and feel like 3 years out? What do you see, experience, or feel? What do your students, staff, or clients say?

Vivid Vision Checklist

1. **Personal**

   ◆ How do YOU spend your time when not at work?
   ◆ What do you want to experience in your family?
   ◆ What are 4–5 words that describe you at your best and what routines will get you there? (**Need help?**

Check out this resource: https://betterleadersbetter schools.com/live-at-your-best/)

- What is your WHY?
- Bucket list?
- Anything else?

2. **Organizational**

- What do you see?
- What do you hear?
- School: What are your staff, students, parents saying?
- School: What programs do you offer students and the community?
- Who makes up your team?
- How would you describe your culture?
- What does the local media, blogs, and social media write about you?
- What do your employees discuss at the water cooler?
- What is the buzz about you in your community?
- What is your marketing like?
- How is the organization running day-to-day?
- What do YOU do everyday? Are you focused on strategy, team building, community relationships, etc.?
- What does your school budget look like?
- What programs are funded now? What are your priorities?
- How are your core values being realized among your employees?
- Anything else?

3. **How do I do this in a school?**

- Make a draft
- Bring to key leaders
- Revise
- Bring to staff
- Revise
- Bring to community
- Revise and publish

4. Template: Cover EVERY aspect of your organization. Go here to steal a template I made for you: https://better leadersbetterschools.com/vision-template. The template is filled out with ideas I created for myself and the companies I run. It is created in Google Docs so feel free to "make a copy" or download as a word document and edit as needed.

In Closing . . .

I hope this second volume of *EdWriteNow* has inspired you to go deeper and take action on using the idea of "Connection" to build stronger relationships and create a world class school culture.

The authors humbly ask you to tag us on Twitter and use the hashtag #EdWriteNow to keep the conversation going. In fact, right now, put down this book and tell us what was your BIGGEST takeaway from the text? We'd love to know and encourage you along the way!

49971187R00109

Made in the USA
Columbia, SC
29 January 2019